HUMAN RESOURCE MANAGEMENT

FOR BBA (3RD SEMESTER) OF BHAGAT PHOOL SINGH WOMEN'S UNIVERSITY, KHANPUR

ANNU SEHRAWAT

Copyright © Annu Sehrawat
All Rights Reserved.

ISBN 979-888546449-9

This book has been published with all efforts taken to make the material error-free after the consent of the author. However, the author and the publisher do not assume and hereby disclaim any liability to any party for any loss, damage, or disruption caused by errors or omissions, whether such errors or omissions result from negligence, accident, or any other cause.

While every effort has been made to avoid any mistake or omission, this publication is being sold on the condition and understanding that neither the author nor the publishers or printers would be liable in any manner to any person by reason of any mistake or omission in this publication or for any action taken or omitted to be taken or advice rendered or accepted on the basis of this work. For any defect in printing or binding the publishers will be liable only to replace the defective copy by another copy of this work then available.

THE CONSTITUTION OF INDIA

PREAMBLE

WE, THE PEOPLE OF INDIA, having solemnly

resolved to constitute INDIA into a SOVEREIGN

SOCIALIST SECULAR DEMOCRATIC REPUBLIC

and to secure to all its citizens:

JUSTICE , social , economic and political ;

LIBERTY of thoughts , expression , belief faith and worship ;

EQUALITY of status and of opportunity ;

and to promote among them all ;

FRATERNITY assuring the dignity of the individual and the unity and
Integrity of the nation ;

WE DO HEREBY GIVE TO OURSELVES THIS CONSTITUTION.

Contents

Contents

Foreword

BPS University, KHABPUR has revised the course contents of BBA course. This book has been especially written for the new syllabus of paper code : BBA 209 "Human Resource Management". Some of the distinguishing features of the book are as follows :

- Full coverage of the prescribed syllabus.
- Systematic and sequential arrangement of topics as per the syllabus.
- Lucid and simple language.

I am sure that this book would be very useful both students and teachers. Suggestions and critical comments for improvement of the book are welcome.

Author : Annu Sehrawat

Acknowledgements

I would like to express my special thanks of gratitude to my Teacher **"Dr. Prashant Kumar & Mr. Kapil"** as well as our Principal **"Mr. Dinesh Singh "** who gave me the golden opportunity to do this wonderful work "write a book" , which also helped me in doing a lot of Research and i came to know about so many new things. I am really thankful to them.

Secondly, I would also like to thank my **PARENTS** and friends who helped me.

Author : Annu Sehrawat

Studies at Bachelor of Business Administration (2nd year)

Management Department (GCW GOHANA)

Website: annusehrawat8520.blogspot.com

E-Mail : annusehrawat8520@gmail.com

Prologue

SYLLABUS
BPS UNIVERSITY, KHANPUR
BBA (3rd Semester)
Human Resource Management
Paper Code : BBA - 209

UNIT - 1

Nature, Scope, Objectives and Functions of HRM, Evolution of HRM, Changing Trends in HRM, Strategic Planning and HRM (SHRM): Meaning, Features, Difference Between SHRM and HRM. HRP: Concept, Need and Importance of HRP, Factors affecting HRP, Human Resource Planning Process.

UNIT- 2

Job Analysis : Meaning and Objective, Process, Methods of collecting data, Uses of job analysis, Problem of job analysis. Recruiment and Selection : meaning and factors governing recruitment, Recruitment sources and techniques. Meaning and process of Selection, Problem associated with Recruitment and Selection. Job Evaluation : Meaning, process and Methods of Job Evalution.

UNIT - 3

Employee Retention: Meaning, Factors responsible for high employee turnover, Employee Retention strategies. HR Training and Development : Concept, Need, Process of Training and Development Programme. Methods of Training Programme and levels of Training Evaluation, Impediments to effective Training.

UNIT-4

Performance Appraisal: Meaning, Purpose, Essentials of Effective Performance Appraisal System, Various

Components of Performance Appraisal, Methods and techniques of Performance Appraisal. Managing Compensationand Employee Remuneration: Concept, objectives, Components of Employee Remuneration, Fctor Influencing Employee Remuneratio, Challenges of Remuneration. Incentives : Concept, Importance and Process of Incentives. Fringe Benefits: Meaning, Forms and Administration of Benefit.

CHAPTER ONE

Nature of HRM

What is Human Resource Management (HRM)?

Human resource management (HRM) is the process of acquiring, training, appraising, and compensating employees, and of attending to their labour relations, health and safety, and fairness concerns.

HRM Definition

According to M L Cuming, "Human Resource Management is concerned with obtaining the best possible staff for an organization and having got them looking after them so that they want to stay and give their best to their jobs."

Dale Yoder defines Human Resource Management as that part of the phase of management dealing effectively with control and use of manpower as distinguished from other sources of power.

According to F. E. L. Brech, Human Resource Management is that part of management progress which is primarily concerned with the human constituents of an organization.

Edison defines Human Resource Management as the science of human engineering.

According to Leon C. Megginson, the term human resource can be thought of as, "the total knowledge, skill, creative abilities, talents and aptitudes of an Organization's workforce, as well as the values, attitudes and beliefs of the individuals involved."

Nature of HRM

<u>What is HRM</u> Nature? Human resource management aims at fulfilling the goal of each individual and the organization on a whole.

Nature of HRM are:

1. <u>Pervasive Force</u>
2. <u>People Oriented</u>
3. <u>Action-Oriented</u>
4. <u>Future-Oriented</u>
5. <u>Development Oriented</u>
6. <u>Enhance Employee Relations</u>
7. <u>Interdisciplinary Function</u>

Nature of <u>human resource management</u> are:

Pervasive Force

Human Resource Management is an inherent part of an organization. It is pervasive in nature and present in all enterprises at all levels of management. It is the responsibility of each manager to select the right candidate under him and pay attention to the development and satisfaction of each sub-ordinate.

People Oriented

Human Resource Management focuses on and values people at work both as individuals and groups. It encourages people to develop their full potential and in return give the best to the organization.

Action-Oriented

Human Resource Management does follow rules, records, and policies but it stresses the action. The focus is on providing an effective and timely solution to employees for any problems, tensions, or controversies faced by them.

Future-Oriented

To sustain and grow in this competitive environment organizations follow long term strategic planning. Effective Human Resource Management prepares people for current as well as future challenges, especially working in an environment characterized by dramatic changes.

Development Oriented

HRM continuously works towards the development of employees. There are various tools used to make the employees reach their maximum potential. Training programs are held to help employees enhance their skills and knowledge. Monetary and non-monetary reward structures are tuned to motivate the employees.

Enhance Employee Relations

HRM helps to build a healthy relationship between the employees at various levels. It encourages mentoring and counseling to help employees in times of need. It aims at creating a culture in the organization that is conducive to learning and growth.

Interdisciplinary Function

The knowledge that has influenced Human Resource Management is interdisciplinary in nature. It drives knowledge from five major bodies: education, system theory, economics, psychology, and organizational behaviour.

Scope of HRM

What is HRM Scope? Human Resource management has a very wide scope, Every department and activity in an organization needs human resources, even if it is about running machinery.

The scope of human resource management can be broadly divided into three:

1. **HRM in Personnel Management**
2. **HRM in Employee Welfare**
3. **HRM in Industrial Relation**

HRM in Personnel Management

The objective here is to ensure the individual growth of each employee which indirectly contributes to the overall growth of the entire organization.

HRM in Employee Welfare

This aspect of HRM is concerned with the working condition and the amenities at the workplace. It makes the environment worth working by eliminating workplace hazards, providing job safety, medical and health services etc.

HRM in Industrial Relation

The main aim of this aspect is to maintain peace and harmony in the organization. It requires effective interaction with the labour or employee unions, sensitively addressing their grievances and settling their disputes.

Objectives of HRM

The primary <u>objective of HRM</u> is to place a competent and willing workforce in the right position and at the right time.

Further, it aims to obtain maximum individual development, desirable working conditions and at the same time, it focuses on contributing to the realization of the organizational goals.

The main <u>objectives of HRM are:</u>

- **To help the organization achieve its goals:** HRM is the means to assist the organization to achieve its goals. It ensures effective utilization of Human Resources which in turn results in the efficient utilization of all the other organizational resources.
- **To employ a skilled workforce and focus on their training and development:** HRM aims at employing the skills and abilities of the workforce efficiently. It

generates maximum development of Human Resources within the organization by offering opportunities for growth to employees through training and development.

- **To ensure employee job satisfaction and maintain a quality of work-life**: HRM focuses on fulfilling the personal objectives of the employees which helps in enhancing their contribution to the organization. Their objective is to ensure respect for human beings by providing various services and welfare facilities to the personnel.

Societal Objective: HRM must ensure that there is compliance with the legal and ethical standards of the society at each level and function of the organization. It implies that organizations manage human resources in an ethical and socially responsible manner.

CHAPTER TWO

Function and Importance of HRM

<u>Functions of HRM</u> are:

1. <u>HR Planning</u>
2. <u>Job Analysis and Design</u>
3. <u>Recruitment and Selection</u>
4. <u>Orientation and Placement</u>
5. <u>Training and Development</u>

HR Planning

Human Resource Planning is a process that identifies current and future human resource needs for an organization to achieve its goals.

Job Analysis and Design

Job Analysis is the determination of the precise characteristics of a job through an in-depth and detailed examination of the activities to be performed.

Job design allows job analysis. It involves designing the content of a job, it combines the tasks into a job to be assigned to an individual and further fixes the duties and responsibilities to do the job.

Recruitment and Selection

Recruitment is the process of searching the best-qualified candidate from within or outside the organization in a cost-effective manner.

Orientation and Placement

Orientation is the process in which the new employees are introduced and made familiar to their jobs, complex processes, coworkers, and organizations. Placement includes assigning tasks to new employees and the promotion or transfer of present employees.

Training and Development

Training is the process of enhancing the knowledge and skill of an employee required for a particular job.
Development is an ongoing and continuous process that aims at improving the personality and attitude of employees.

1. Analyze and create new HR policies: The major responsibility of the HR manager is to plan appropriate human resource policies for his organization and implement them.

2. Interview arrangement and perfect employee selection: Procurement and selection of efficient and skills human resources is another important function of human resource management.

3. Planning employee Placement: Procured human resources should be given proper guidance and they should be placed at the desired position and place.

4. The arrangement of a training program for a new employee: An employee should be trained for a better performance after recruiting and placing. Training will change employee's knowledge, way of working, attitudes toward work, and interaction with their co-workers.

5. Transfer and Promotion: Through promotion employees get higher salaries and status. Through transfer, employees may be placed at the proper position as desired by either the employees or the employer. Promotion work like an incentive to employees & this is essential for organizational improvement.

6. Analysis of Job: Analysis of a job is one kind of systematic exploration of the activities within a job. It will define the duties, responsibilities, and accountability of a job.

7. Ensure working environment: Thisis an essential part of human resource management and this is a must for every organization. It may bring benefits for the employer like an increase in productivity, a positive attitude to coworkers, and organization.

8. Employees Protection: Employees should be well protected. Without safety measures, the human resources of the organization will not perform well/properly. This is one of the most important functions of human resource management.

9. Remuneration: This is one of the prime functions of human resource management. Human resources should be given to provide reasonable remuneration to work properly.

10. Employee services: They should be given service packages to work properly. Employee services increase the satisfaction of employees, attract and retain them to the organization for a long time.

11. Evaluation of merit and Job: You can't judge anyone's efficiency without job evaluation. So employee's jobs should be properly evaluated by placing them at the proper position of the organ gram. Similarly, merit rating is done by selecting the employees for offering benefits packages.

12. Labor management relation: To be a successful organization HR should maintain labor-management relations. There is a need for a good and harmonious organizational goal.

13. EnsureWorkers Participation: HR should ensure worker participation when they take the decision and formulate rules and regulations and this the best practice in the age of democracy in the organization.

14. Agreement with Trade Unions: Now a day's trade unions are very powerful in the industrial context. So, HR authority can't run the organization properly without satisfying trade union leaders.

15. Leadership and cooperation: An organization needs a proper leader to run properly. And a leader needs co-operation to utilize the resources perfectly.

16. Responsible for giving rewards and benefits: Human resource department is responsible for giving rewards and befits to get a better response from human resources.

17. Maintaining discipline: Discipline is essential for an organization to work properly. H.R. managers should take proper disciplinary action indiscriminately when indiscipline arises.

18. Career Planning and Development of employee: The HR Manager should try to plan for the development of the career of its human resource. Career means the pattern of work-related experiences that span the course of personal life, Career development looks at the long-term career effectiveness and success of organizational personnel.

19. Handling Grievances: This is the responsibility of the HR manager to handle all grievances.

20. Reviewing employee needs: This can help the employees to realize that management gives them importance.

Importance of HRM

The <u>Importance of human resource management</u> can be discussed at three levels:

1. <u>Instrument for growth to an organization</u>
2. <u>Liaison between the employee and employer</u>
3. <u>Professional field</u>

Instrument for growth to an organization

The survival and growth of the organization depend largely on the competence and its effective management. Human resource management makes workers efficient and motivated through training, supervision, and inspiring leadership.

Liaison between the employee and employer

It tries to maintain the balance between the available jobs and the job seekers according to their needs and organizational requirement.

Its significance can also be determined by the elimination of wastages and providing a healthy and conducive environment for employee growth.

Professional field

Human Resource Management has moved to a specialist function. The realization of employee goals is the sole responsibility, as a specialist function.

Its focus has moved from employee management to employee development. The skills development and individual capacity utilization are the challenges faced by human resource managers in the current scenario.

1. **Formulation of HR policies:** For the proper formulation of human resource policies knowledge and efficiency on human resource management required.

2. **Implementation of HR Policies:** Not only formulation rather an implementation of HR policies signify the importance of HR management in an industrial organization.

3. **Review of employee needs:** human resources management suggest proper action by reviewing employee

need. And it increases the efficiency of an organization.

4. Development of social welfare: If human resource management (HRM) is welfare-oriented for employees, some development of social welfare may take place.

5. Utilization of Human Resources: HRM can show it's important by proper utilization of human resources after getting everything done by employees.

6. Development of Labor-Management Relations: Good labor-management relation is essential for a peaceful working environment. Human resources management can ensure it.

7. Overall development of organization: Human Resources management can play a significant role in achieving productivity and profitability targets. Thus it can help the overall development of the organization.

CHAPTER THREE

Human Resource Man

Skills and Proficiency of HR Managers

Job of an HR manager is the most challenging one as there is no factor of production as complex as people. HR managers need to integrate processes, people and technology in an efficient and effective manner that should enable the organization to achieve its goals.

While doing all this they need to assess, develop, reward and retain a wide variety of people. Discussed below are the skill sets that an efficient HR manager should possess

- <u>Multi- knowledgeable</u>
- <u>Personal attributes</u>
- <u>Professional attitude</u>
- <u>Ethical attitude</u>

Multi- knowledgeable

HR managers should possess knowledge of all the diverse fields that collectively run a business. Since HR management is required in all the departments and at all levels, it is important that HR managers should be competent in all the diverse areas of finance, sales, marketing, operations etc

Personal attributes

HR managers should possess the mental ability to communicate, articulate and handle people and situations with intelligence He should have the learning skills as he needs to continuously upgrade himself to stay abreast with the outside world.

Coaching and teaching is a continuous process that an HR professional undertakes to develop the employee's skills and personality.

HR managers should have both leadership and executive skills. They should be able to lead a large group of people towards a course of action that is in the best interest of the individual as well as the organization. They should also accurately and quickly execute the management's decision regarding personal issues.

Professional attitude

HR manager's job is getting professionalized. He should be organized as there is no margin of error when dealing with the lives and careers of people. He should have a comprehensive understanding of HR policies, principles, programs, practices and laws.

Ethical attitude

For healthy and successful running of a business, it is very important that the HR managers comply with the code of moral principles and values with respect to what is right or wrong. Employees should be coached from time to time and their ethical dilemmas should be cleared.

In case of any violation, the company should not hesitate to punish the unethical behaviour of the employees. HR professionals should communicate clearly and fairly and aim to promote equity. HR professionals are company conscience and keepers of confidential information. They should respect and maintain privacy always.

Human Resource Manager Competency

Professor Dave Ulrich and his colleagues say that today's human resource managers need the knowledge, skills, and competencies to be:

- **Talent Managers/Organization Designers**, with a mastery of traditional human resource management tasks such as acquiring, training, and compensating employees.
- **Culture and Change Stewards**, able to create human resource practices that support the firms cultural values.
- **Strategy Architects**, with the skills to help establish the company s overall strategic plan, and to put in place the human resource practices required to support accomplishing that plan.
- **Operational Executors**, able to anticipate, draft, and implement the human resource practices (for instance in testing and appraising) the company needs to implement its strategy.
- **Business Allies**, competent to apply business knowledge (for instance in finance, sales, and

production) that enable them to help functional and general managers to achieve their departmental goals.

- **Credible Activists**, with the leadership and other competencies that make them both credible (respected, admired, listened to) and active (offers a point of view, takes a position, challenges assumptions.)

Why is Human Resource Management Important to all Managers?

These concepts and techniques are important to all managers for several reasons.

- **Avoid personnel mistakes**: first, having a command of this knowledge will help you avoid the sorts of personnel mistakes you don't want to make while managing.
- **Improve profits and performance**: similarly, effective human Resource management can help ensure that you get results through people.

CHAPTER FOUR

HR Tech

Greater use of technology has led to organizational use of a human resource management system (HRMS), which is an integrated system providing information used by HR management in decision making. This terminology emphasizes that making HR decisions, not just building databases and using technology, is the primary reason for compiling data in an information system.

Purposes for Expanding HR Technology

The rapid expansion of HR technology serves two major purposes in organizations. One relates to administrative and operational efficiency, and the other to effectiveness.

Improve the Efficiency

The first purpose is to improve the efficiency with which data on employees and HR activities are compiled. The most basic example is the automation of payroll and benefits activities. Another common use of technology is tracking EEO/ affirmative action activities.

Beyond those basic applications, the use of Web-based information systems has allowed the HR unit in organizations to become more administratively efficient and communicate more quickly to employees.

Strategic HR Planning

The second purpose of the use of HR technology is related to strategic HR planning. Having accessible data enables HR planning and managerial decision making to be based to a greater degree on information rather than relying on managerial perceptions and intuition.

HR Certification

As the human resource manager s job becomes more demanding, human resource managers are becoming more professional. More than 115,000 HR professionals have already passed one or more of the Society for Human Resource Management (SHRM) HR professional certification exams. SHRM s Human Resource Certification Institute offers these exams.

The Evolution of HRM (Human Resource Management)

Human Resource Management(HRM), being the department responsible for maintaining discipline, has come a long way. The term HRM is relatively a very new term for handling employees in every organization. It is still evolving and will keep on evolving to keep up with the changing world.

The evolution of <u>human resource management</u>(hrm) terms is of very recent origin. It began revolving around the 1980s. During the ancient period, for a long time goods were produced mainly by skilled craftsmen and artisans. They were responsible for handling all the processes, generating it, producing it, and finally selling it. Let us have a look at how the evolution of the concept of hrm came into existence.

Evolution of HRM- The Industrial Revolution

Managing workers at companies began at the time of the Industrial Revolution during the late eighteenth century. Before this era, many large organizations existed, but without the advanced technology, it was hard to maintain them. During this time, the work atmosphere was very unfavorable and the employees used to put in endless hours in the company for very little pay.

FW Taylor introduced scientific management in the twentieth century. He gathered that there was 'one best way' to handle every role in every company to make it run more efficiently and smoothly. Taylor examined the job and narrowed it down into essential elements, i.e. job specialization.

He believed that employees could be trained at one job role to become an expert, but he completely ignored the fact that doing the same job every day will get boring and mundane for the employees. During this Revolution, science and technology started being applied to all elements of work in modern industries. This affected every Human Resource management system in many ways such as-

• The area of the job for all the employees changed from their home to a common area, where everyone performed tasks under the same roof. The production techniques evolved from manual to machines.

• The introduction of mechanization made the work so easy that even women and kids started to get employed.

• With the help of computer technology, controlling industrial activities became very productive and efficient. Inventory control, production control, method control, manpower control, and financial control had all become very efficient with the introduction of computerized procedures.

• The expanded use of machines resulted in a vast change in employment. Working the machinery required skilled knowledge, which many employees did not have. This ended up making them unemployed and helpless.

In conclusion, the Industrial Revolution brought about discipline, monotony, materialism, job displacement, work interdependence, and impersonality. In economic terms, the revolution increased the accumulation of capital and goods to a large extent.

Consequently, commerce and business were highly accelerated, entrepreneurs and owners performed well, but the average citizen poorly failed

Evolution of HRM (Human Resource Management)- Period of Trade Unionism

Soon after the factory system surfaced, many employees began to get together to discuss their common dilemmas. Every employee was forced to work for long hours under dangerous conditions, for practically no wage. This encouraged the employees to join together and protest to prove their worth and importance to an organization.

They used different kinds of techniques like strike, walkouts, slowdowns, boycotts, picketing, and sabotage. Even physical force was used at times. This, however, proved to be a success, as without the employees the companies would come crashing down. The employers were forced to listen to every demand of all the employees.

New organizational units were created especially to deal with the method improvements, the study of wages, and more attention was paid to the needs of every employee.

Evolution and development of HRM- Social Responsibility

As seen above, the earlier employers were not sympathetic towards their workers and their needs. With time, they started to realize the importance of every employee and started giving them the importance that they deserve. The companies started creating a positive work environment where the employees were satisfied and hence started showing more productivity.

Labour laws were renewed according to which child labor was abolished. The workers were given proper training on how to use the machinery. High wages and good working conditions helped the workers in being more productive, which in turn contributed to the growth of a company.

Evolution and growth of HRM- Scientific management

The scientific management era began in 1900 and reached its peak by 1930. It was a major revolution and thus has managed to stay somewhat alive to date. Handling everything manually was getting exhausting for the employees and was hampering their productivity and efficiency.

There was a need to introduce new advanced technology which would eliminate the burden on the employees. Employees used to perform slowly as they used to think that if they performed at a fast pace, it would result in a grave error, which could cost them their jobs. This resulted in plenty of time wastage and loss of productivity. Employees were forced to take up jobs outside of their comfort zone and skills.

Not having knowledge about that field, hampered the credibility of an employee as well as the company. Thus, Taylor introduced the best way to solve this, by picking the right man for the right job. By putting the suited employee for the right job with the correct tools, companies were able to make significant improvements in productivity. This was done by offering the employees great economic incentives and higher daily wages.

To boost up the morale of every employee, the reward and appraisal system was introduced. This created a healthy competitive environment by encouraging employees to perform harder to achieve rewards. Scientific management included a lot of essential elements such as-

• *Task planning*

Scientific task planning entails the total number of hours an employee can perform every day, which is called a fair day's work. The management decides in advance what task needs to be done by which employee and within what amount of time. The final goal is to make maximum utilization of resources available in a timely sequence to promote maximum productivity and efficiency.

• *Time study*

Time and motion studies were introduced to avoid wastage of time and resources. The same task was given to different employees, and the hours are taken by everyone to complete it was noted. This helped in taking out the average time required to complete a particular task. Fatigue studies were also conducted, where the boredom and monotony caused due to a particular task were noted.

• *Standardization*

Various standards were set up in advance to ensure that the employees are clear about the objective and target. It was also used to avoid wastage of resources and improving the work quality.

• *Wages bottomed on productivity-*

To ensure that the employees are giving their best and not taking advantage of the resources, wages were given out based on work done in the lowest amount of time. According to this, an employee who finishes the entire work on time gets paid a higher wage than the worker who doesn't complete the task at a given time. This creates a sense of healthy competition, ensuring that the employees give their best to earn a maximum wage.

Evolution of Human Resource Management-Introduction to HRM

As time changes, the techniques need to change too. With the coming of advanced technology, a need for a better system emerged to handle the employees in every organization successfully. Over the years the HRM evolution concept has increased and is continuing to do so.

The integration of HR management in businesses is a tried and tested method to improve productivity and increase efficiency. With the numerous benefits of human resource management, many companies are taking advantage of it, and needless to say, are very happy with the outcome. With the increase in the number of companies and their employees, a single person could not handle the administrative tasks of everyone in the organization.

Human Resource Management was created to develop and handle all the tasks systematically and efficiently. Right from attracting candidates, to their recruitment, onboarding, and retention. Everything is now handled by a human resource department. The three key responsibilities of HR is-

• Recruitment

In today's competitive business world, recruitment has become a wearying task. Recruitment companies are competing with each other neck-to-neck, to find the best potential candidate for their firms. For any job role, there are numerous applicants. It is the responsibility of human resources to find the perfect candidate for their company.

• *Onboarding*

When new hires join the organization, they have expectations and aspirations for their job. The human resource department ensures that the onboarding of every new hire is easy and seamless. They introduce an employee to the rules and regulations of the company and make sure that the goals and targets of the new hires are aligned with that of the organization.

• *Retention*

The most important role of the human resource department is to make sure that their best employees are happy and satisfied with their jobs. They don't want the company to lose a crucial asset. Human resource organizes various activities and gives appraisals and rewards to the deserving employees. This helps the employees in being satisfied by their job, thus helping the company to retain them for the long haul.

Thus, the **evolution and growth of HRM (human resource management) have come a long way.** With the advanced technology and software, managing the employees in every organization has become smooth sailing for human resources.

Pocket HRMS is a new-age HR software with integrated modules supporting functions of human resource management.

top trends of Human Resource Management

top trends of Human Resource Management

- **Promote Diversity and Inclusion**

Company culture plays a pivotal role to provide a positive experience to its employees. With employees belonging to diverse races, ages, genders, sexual orientations, and cultures, industries ought to make their employees feel that they belong to a community.

HR professionals need to plant a seed of inclusion and affiliation where the employees feel confident to express their ideas with equity. Research shows that a cohesive work culture boosted employee performance to 56% and decreased turnover risk to 50%. Motivate them to be involved in the company vision holistically.

- **The Trend of Work From Home (WFH)**

The Coronavirus pandemic has altered the paradigms of business domains worldwide. This global overnight shift to remote work puts a high value on flexible work arrangements. Four out of five HR managers believe the move to working remotely has caused less employee absenteeism, with employees available online when needed.

In 2021, many corporations are offering remote-work as a full-time opportunity. With this, HR departments need to adapt to new workplace settings to keep the employees engaged and on track.

• Cultivate Critical Thinking, Soft Skills, Digital Skills

Gone are the days when education and job skills were the only criteria for the recruitment of employees. The 21st century calls for HR personnel to look for a combination of power skills in the workforce. Search for applicants with digital skills like data analytics and digital literacy.

Assess critical thinking skills like strategic thinking and conflict management. Soft skills like emotional intelligence and creativity are considered a priority by businesses these days for the humanistic work environment. Choose candidates with learnability and aptitude to operate in a tech-human blended work mode.

• Employee Wellness Programs

With the fast-paced work culture and competitive race, stress levels of employees have been on the rise. To keep their mental health intact, HR practitioners should advance workplace wellness programs to strengthen employee's wellbeing to have a work-life balance. Build motivated, engaged, and loyal employees who are cared for and nurtured.

Some activities to conduct can include healthy lunches, team building activities, site fitness classes, counseling sessions, festive celebrations, and weekly interactive video calls. Educate your employees about mental health issues like depression, anxiety, and stress and how to handle them.

- ## Artificial Intelligence (AI) and Machine Learning

AI-based algorithms such as applicant tracking software, combined with an increase in cloud-computing, can assist HR professionals in the recruitment of candidates and streamline workflow. AI tools promote merit-based selection eliminating conscious or unconscious bias.

AI aids HR to manage onboarding, integration, employee training, performance, reporting, payroll, and data administration. Integrate Robotic process automation (RPA) to encompass skills like chatbots, natural language processing (NLP), and machine learning to access the data.

- ## Creativity in Recruitment and Learning Management System (LMS) for Training

HR specialists often complain about the challenge of hiring talented employees. They need to adapt to creative ways to select qualified applicants or the positions they need to fill. Apart from AI, talent acquisition teams can maneuver headhunting firms or recruitment marketing agencies to find potential candidates.

Assimilate learning management system or tools to facilitate training and workshops To cultivate future talent via the internet. Some LMS include Bridge, GoSkills, Absorb, and Moodle. Further, incorporate mentoring programs to escalate the retention rates of the employees.

- **Train the Workforce with Virtual Reality (VR) and Augmented Reality (AR)**

With the advent of digital integration, every department, including HR, is wielding the best of novel technologies like VR and AR for employee growth and hands-on experience. They have become go-to training methods for a multitude of organizations such as insurance, customer service, retail, construction, and safety training, to name a few.

The practical learning fostered by them is seen in some training programs to effectively bring about behavioral changes in trainees for them to develop new skills needed for their new job. They also contribute to front-end processes like recruiting and onboarding.

- **Fluid Task Management with Gig Economy**

HR staff should know that the younger generations prefer work-life balance with flexible schedules and Telecommuting. The gig economy where people like to work independently is witnessing a sharp spike as people are increasingly looking to work on their terms and conditions.

Employees are opting out of the 9-5 work schedule to side hustle in addition to day jobs. Others, like freelancers and consultants, like to work for themselves 100% of the time. HR practitioners and team leaders must look for new ways to keep their working forces efficient and agile with this changing trend.

A company operates by its workforce. That's why it's not only essential for the HR professionals to search for the best talents but also try to create a work environment that makes them loyal to your organization. Enhance employee experience, provide continuous learning and skills development programs to upscale your company's reputation, and make your company ideal for young job seekers.

CHAPTER SIX

What is Strategic Human Resource management (SHRM)?

Strategic human resource management is the connection between a company's human resources and its strategies, objectives, and goals. The aim of strategic human resource management is to:

- Advance flexibility innovation, and competitive advantage.
- Develop a fit for purpose organizational culture.
- Improve business performance.

In order for strategic human resource management to be effective, <u>human resources</u> (HR) must play a vital role as a strategic partner when company policies are created and implemented. Strategic HR can be demonstrated throughout different activities, such as hiring, training and rewarding employees.

Strategic HR involves looking at ways that human resources can make a direct impact on a company's growth. HR personnel need to adopt a strategic approach to developing and retaining employees to meet the needs of the company's long-term plans.

HR issues can be a difficult hurdle to cross for many companies, there are all kinds of different components that can confuse business owners and cause them to make ineffective decisions that slow down the operations for their employees as well as their business. HR departments that practice strategic human resource management do not work independently within a silo; they interact with other departments within an organization in order to understand their goals and then create strategies that align with those objectives, as well as those of the organization. As a result, the goals of a human resource department reflect and support the goals of the rest of the organization. Strategic HRM is seen as a partner in organizational success, as opposed to a necessity for legal compliance or compensation. Strategic HRM utilizes the talent and opportunity within the human resources department to make other departments stronger and more effective.

Why is strategic human resource management important?

Companies are more likely to be successful when all teams are working towards the same objectives. Strategic HR carries out analysis of employees and determines the actions required to increase their value to the company. Strategic human resource management also uses the results of this analysis to develop HR techniques to address employee weaknesses.

The following are benefits of strategic human resource management:

- Increased job satisfaction.
- Better work culture.

- Improved rates of customer satisfaction.
- Efficient resource management.
- Proactive approach to managing employees.
- Boost productivity.

Seven steps to strategic human resource management
Strategic human resource management is key for the retention and development of quality staff. It's likely that employees will feel valued and want to stay with a company that places a premium on employee retention and engagement. Before implementing strategic human resource management, you will need to create a strategic HR planning process using the steps below:

- Develop a thorough understanding of company's objectives
- Evaluate HR capability
- Analyze current HR capacity in light of your goals
- Estimate company's future HR requirements
- Determine the tools required for employees to complete the job
- Implement the human resource management strategy
- Evaluation and corrective action

Strategic human resource management is important for every company. Company doesn't need to employ a specific number of employees before start to consider implementing strategic human resource management principles. In fact, if we have a plan to grow business, we should be thinking about linking this growth to strategic human resource management. Some companies outsource this part of their business because they don't have an in-house HR function. Strategic human resource services provide full-service HR functions including developing a human resource management strategy. Strategic HR services help to take away the burden of both operational and strategic management to facilitate the growth of your business.

Seven Consultancy is a result of the motivation of young entrepreneurship under the guidance of experienced professional from industry. Young entrepreneurs know the recent trends of market. Flexibility of the services has helped Seven Consultancy to secure a brand name in the market. We have access to an overall Human Resource Solution (HR Consultancy). Seven Consultancy believes in shaping the way of success for its clients.

Our Consultancy are specialized in Recruitment, Placement, Manpower & Job Consultancy. We are one of the Top HR Consultant in Mumbai, Navi Mumbai & Thane. We have well defined customized HR solution for different segments. We have received awards as Best HR Consultancy in Mumbai.

Characteristics of Strategic Human Resource Management

1. **Recognition of the outside Environment:** Outside environment presents some opportunities and threats to the organization in the form of-

- Laws
- Economic conditions
- Social and demographic change
- Domestic and international political forces

- Technology and so on.

A strategic human resource strategy explicitly recognizes the threats and opportunities in each area and attempts to capitalize on the opportunities while minimizing or deflecting the effect of threats.

2. The impact of Competition: The forces of competition in attracting, rewarding, and using employees have a major effect on corporate human resource strategy. Forces play out in local, regional, and national labor markets.

Labor market dynamics of wage rates, unemployment rates, working conditions, benefits levels minimum wage legislation, and competition reputation all have an impact on and are affected by strategic human resource decisions.

3. Long-range Focus: A strategic human resource management should be long-range focus cause this is not easy to change the strategic human resource policy.

4. Choice and decision-making focus: In other words, the strategy has a problem solving or problem preventing focus. The strategy concentrates on the question, "what should the organization do and why?" this action orientation requires that decisions be made and carried out.

5. Consideration of all personnel: A strategic approach to human resources is concerned with all of the firm's employees, not just its hourly or operational personnel. Traditionally, human resource management focuses on hourly employees, with most clerical exempt employees also included.

6. Integration with the corporate strategy: Human resource strategy adopted by a firm should be integrated with the firm's corporate strategy.

The key idea behind overall strategic mgt is to coordinate all of the company's resources, including human resources; in such a way that everything a company does contributes to carrying out its strategy.

Synergy means the extra benefit or value realized when resources have been combined and coordinated effectively.

This concept often referred to as economies of scope, makes the combined whole of the company make valuable than the sum of its parts. It is a true benefit of good strategic management of resources.

CHAPTER SEVEN

Models of human resource management

Models of human resource management

1. Training and Development: Human Resource Management tries to train, and develop its employees considering individual, organization, and training institute need.

2. Organization Development: Organizational development is a systematic process that can be undertaken and some interventions can be practiced for the development of human resources and organizational activities. That can help the proper functioning of the organization.

3. Organization/Job Design: Job / Organization is the most important models of human resource management.

4. Human Resource Planning: Human resource planning focus on arranging the organization's major human resource needs strategies and philosophies.

5. Selection and Staffing: After job design or recruitment, the most appropriate candidates are chosen from available candidates, which is called selection.

6. Personnel Research and information system: its focus assuring and personal information base.

7. Compensation/Benefits: Compensation refers to all the extrinsic rewards that employees in change for their work.

8. Employee Assistance: Its focus assuring providing personal problem solving, counseling to the individual employees.

9. Union/Labor Relations: Labor relations are an essential part of the working environment and industrial peace.

Differences Between HRM and SHRM

The differences between HRM and SHRM can be drawn clearly on the following grounds:

1. The governance of manpower of the organisation in a thorough and structured manner is called Human Resource Management or HRM. A managerial function which implies framing of HR strategies in such a way to direct employees efforts towards the goals of an organisation is known as SHRM.
2. The process of HRM is reactive in nature. On the other hand, SHRM is a proactive management function.
3. In human resource management, the responsibility of manpower lies with the staff specialists, whereas in strategic human resource management, the task of managing the workforce, is vested in the line managers.
4. HRM follows fragmented approach, which stresses on applying management principles while managing people in an organisation. As against this, SHRM follows an integrated approach, which involves lining up of

business strategy with the company's HR practices.

5. Human resource management emphasises on employee relations, ensuring employees motivation, and also the firm conforms to the necessary employment laws. Conversely, SHRM focuses on a partnership with internal and external constituent groups.

6. HRM supports short-term business goals and outcomes, but SHRM supports long-term goals and results of business.

7. In human resource management, the human resource manager plays the role of change follower, i.e. he/she responses to change, hence pursues transactional leadership style. As opposed to SHRM, the human resource manager is a change leader, i.e. an imitator, thus seeks transformational leadership.

8. The primary element in HRM is the capital and products, but people and their knowledge are the building blocks of SHRM.

9. If we talk about accountability, a conventional HRM is a cost centre. Unlike a strategic HRM which is an investment centre.

10. In human resource management, stringent control over employees is exercised. As against this, in strategic human resource management, no such control is imposed, rather the rules for managing manpower is lenient.

CHAPTER EIGHT

Human Resource Planning – Meaning

E.W. Vetter viewed human resource planning as "a process by which an organisation should move from its current manpower position to its desired manpower position. Through planning, management strives to have the right number and right kind of people at the right places at the right time, doing things which result in both the organisation and the individual receiving maximum long-run benefit."

According to Leon C. Megginson human resource planning is "an integrated approach to performing the planning aspects of the personnel function in order to have a sufficient supply of adequately developed and motivated people to perform the duties and tasks required to meet organisational objectives and satisfy the individual needs and goals of organisational members."

Human Resource Planning – Need and Importance:

The following points highlight the need and importance of HRP in the organizations:

I. Assessing Future Personnel Needs:

Whether it is surplus labour or labour shortage, it gives a picture of defective planning or absence of planning in an organization. A number of organizations, especially public sector units (PSUs) in India are facing the problem of surplus labour.

It is the result of surplus labour that the companies later on offer schemes like Voluntary Retirement Scheme (VRS) to eliminate surplus staff. Thus, it is better to plan well about employees in advance. Through HRP, one can ensure the employment of proper number and type of personnel.

II. Foundation for Other HRM Functions:

HRP is the first step in all HRM functions. So, HRP provides the essential information needed for the other HRM functions like recruitment, selection, training and development, promotion, etc.

III. Coping with Change:

Changes in the business environment like competition, technology, government guidelines, global market, etc. bring changes in the nature of the job. This means changes in the demand of personnel, content of job, qualification and experience needed. HRP helps the organization in adjusting to new changes.

IV. Investment Perspective:

As a result of change in the mindset of management, investment in human resources is viewed as a better concept in the long run success of the enterprise. Human assets can increase in value as opposed to physical assets. Thus, HRP is considered important for the proper planning of future employees.

V. Expansion and Diversification Plans:

During the expansion and diversification drives, more employees at various levels are needed. Through proper

HRP, an organization comes to know about the exact requirement of personnel in future plans.

VI. Employee Turnover:

Every organization suffers from the small turnover of labour, sometime or the other. This is high among young graduates in the private sector. This necessitates again doing manpower planning for further recruiting and hiring.

VII. Conformity with Government Guidelines:

In order to protect the weaker sections of the society, the Indian Government has prescribed some norms for organizations to follow. For example, reservations for SC/ST, BC, physically handicapped, ex-servicemen, etc. in the jobs. While planning for fresh candidates, HR manager takes into consideration all the Government guidelines.

VIII. International Expansion Strategies:

International expansion strategies of an organization depend upon HRP. Under International Human Resource Management (IHRM), HRP becomes more challenging. An organization may want to fill the foreign subsidiary's key positions from its home country employees or from host-country or from a third country. All this demands very effective HRP.

IX. Having Highly Talented Manpower Inventory:

Due to changing business environment, jobs have become more challenging and there is an increasing need for dynamic and ambitious employees to fill the positions. Efficient HRP is needed for attracting and retaining well qualified, highly skilled and talented employees.

Human Resource Planning – Objectives:

The main objectives of HRP are:

(i) Proper assessment of human resources needs in future.

(ii) Anticipation of deficient or surplus manpower and taking the corrective action.

(iii) To create a highly talented workforce in the organization.

(iv) To protect the weaker sections of the society.

(v) To manage the challenges in the organization due to modernization, restructuring and re-engineering.

(vi) To facilitate the realization of the organization's objectives by providing right number and types of personnel.

(vii) To reduce the costs associated with personnel by proper planning.

(viii) To determine the future skill requirements of the organization.

(ix) To plan careers for individual employee.

(x) Providing a better view of HR dimensions to top management.

(xi) Determining the training and development needs of employ

Human Resource Plan – Factors:

Several factors affect HRP. These factors can be classified into external factors and internal factors.

External Factors:

i. Government Policies – Policies of the government like labour policy, industrial relations policy, policy towards reserving certain jobs for different communities and sons-of the soil, etc. affect the HRP.

ii. Level of Economic Development – Level of economic development determines the level of HRD in the country and thereby the supply of human resources in the future in the country.

iii. Business Environment – External business environmental factors influence the volume and mix of production and thereby the future demand for human resources.

iv. Level of Technology – Level of technology determines the kind of human resources required.

v. International Factors – International factors like the demand for resources and supply of human resources in various countries.

vi. Outsourcing – Availability of outsourcing facilities with required skills and knowledge of people reduces the dependency on HRP and vice-versa.

Internal Factors:

i. Company policies and strategies – Company policies and strategies relating to expansion, diversification, alliances, etc. determines the human resource demand in terms of quality and quantity.

ii. Human resource policies – Human resources policies of the company regarding quality of human resource, compensation level, quality of work-life, etc., influences human resource plan.

iii. Job analysis – Fundamentally, human resource plan is based on job analysis. Job description and job specification determines the kind of employees required.

iv. Time horizons – Companies with stable competitive environment can plan for the long run whereas the firms with unstable competitive environment can plan for only short- term range.

v. Type and quality of information – Any planning process needs qualitative and accurate information. This is more so with human resource plan; strategic, organisational and specific information.

vi. Company's production operations policy – Company's policy regarding how much to produce and how much to buy from outside to prepare a final product influence the number and kind of people required.

vii. Trade unions – Influence of trade unions regarding number of working hours per week, recruitment sources, etc., affect the HRP.

Human Resource Planning

The **Human Resource Planning** is a process of forecasting the organization's demand for and supply of manpower needs in the near future.

1. **Determining the Objectives of Human Resource Planning**: The foremost step in every process is the determination of the objectives for which the process is to be carried on. The objective for which the manpower planning is to be done should be defined precisely, so as to ensure that a right number of people for the right kind of job are selected.

   The objectives can vary across the several departments in the organization such as the personnel demand may differ in marketing, finance, production, HR department, based on their roles or functions.

2. **Analyzing Current Manpower Inventory**: The next step is to analyze the current manpower supply in the organization through the stored information about the employees in terms of their experience, proficiency,

skills, etc. required to perform a particular job.

Also, the future vacancies can be estimated, so as to plan for the manpower from both the internal (within the current employees) and the external (hiring candidates from outside) sources. Thus, it is to be ensured that reservoir of talent is maintained to meet any vacancy arising in the near future.

3. **Forecasting Demand and Supply of Human Resources:** Once the inventory of talented manpower is maintained; the next step is to match the demand for the manpower arising in the future with the supply or available resources with the organization.

   Here, the required skills of personnel for a particular job are matched with the job description and specification.

4. **Analyzing the Manpower Gaps:** After forecasting the demand and supply, the manpower gaps can be easily evaluated. In case the demand is more than the supply of human resources, that means there is a deficit, and thus, new candidates are to be hired.

   Whereas, if the Demand is less than supply, there arises a surplus in the human resources, and hence, the employees have to be removed either in the form of termination, retirement, layoff, transfer, etc.

5. **Employment Plan/Action Plan:** Once the manpower gaps are evaluated, the action plan is to be formulated accordingly. In a case of a deficit, the firm may go either for recruitment, training, interdepartmental transfer

plans whereas in the case of a surplus, the voluntary retirement schemes, redeployment, transfer, layoff, could be followed.

6. **Training and Development:** The training is not only for the new joinees but also for the existing employees who are required to update their skills from time to time.

After the employment plan, the training programmes are conducted to equip the new employees as well as the old ones with the requisite skills to be performed on a particular job.

7. **Appraisal of Manpower Planning:** Finally, the effectiveness of the manpower planning process is to be evaluated. Here the human resource plan is compared with its actual implementation to ensure the availability of a number of employees for several jobs.

At this stage, the firm has to decide the success of the plan and control the deficiencies, if any.

Thus, human resource planning is a continuous process that begins with the objectives of Human Resource planning and ends with the appraisal or feedback and control of the planning process.

CHAPTER TEN

Job Analysis Meaning & Definition

Job analysis is one of the important terms in human resource. It is a way to determine the nature of the job and the duties employee has to perform. It also provides information about what kind of people should be hired for a particular job profile. It is a systematic way to collect information and make judgment about all the things related to a job.

The process of job analysis is to prepare a document which contains all the job specification and descriptions related to the work performed.

Job Analysis Meaning & Definition

Job analysis works in identifying, compiling and analyzing three main important component of Job i.e. Job Description, Job Specification and Job Evaluation.

The Job Analysis process to conduct a study on the data collected on the job to find out the real human requirement of the Job such as Job activities its attributes and other important tasks required for performing a specific Job.

The Process also helps HRM and allows an organization to indentify the roadmap of Job progression for an employee and their interest in the opportunities available in the job for career advancement and increasing pay and benefits.

What is Job Analysis in HRM?

When any employee joins the organization it is imperative on the part of the employee to have information about the job assigned to him or her. Every job is different in terms of responsibility, difficulties, skills and knowledge required to perform the job. The job analysis in Human Resource Management (HRM) provides clarity about different components of the job and the circumstances in which the job should be performed. It is a study and collection of information related to the operation and responsibility associated with the job there are three important components of job analysis, <u>job description</u> and job specification followed by job evaluation.

Job Analysis process in HRM helps to identify the requirement of job and describe the suitability of a person who is supposed to perform the job. Information of job analysis is used in order to prepare job description and specification. It is also utilized to design organization structure, proper recruitment device and selection method along with compensation offered for the job. Further the performance appraisal, training and development facilities, career path counseling and health related conditions are also determined based on the job analysis.

How to Conduct Job analysis?

The answer to how to conduct a job analysis is not an easy one. There are various aspects which are involved while HR department conducts the job analysis. Here the six important aspects which has to utilized while conducting job analysis-

1. Source of data

The source of data is the person or agency which provides information about the ground reality of the job. It includes the job analyst, employees who have experience in performing such job and supervisors who can convey the need of job.

2. Method of collecting data

It is difficult to collect all the information about the job without using any tools. Thus one should conduct interviews of employees and supervisors; questionnaire can be distributed to get exact information about the job. Other information gathering methods includes the records of organization and observation by the agents or managers.

3. Job data

The collected job data should include information related to job such as tasks, performance, standards, responsibilities, knowledge required, skills required, experience needed, job context, equipment used and duties of job holder.

4. Job specification

The job data is then divided into job specification which includes skill requirement, physical demands, knowledge requirement, and abilities needed

5. Job description

The job description is collection of information about tasks, duties and responsibilities of the job holder.

6. Functions of HR department

Once the job description and specification is properly defined the information is used to carry out different HR functions such as recruitment, selection, training and development, performance appraisal and compensation management.

Job Analysis Process & Steps

Job analysis is a very useful tool from the HR point of view, but it is difficult to execute. It involves five steps which have to be followed for favorable end result. The steps are represented in the figure given below-

1. Organizational Job Analysis:

The pertinent information regarding the job is obtained at organizational level. It is critical to know what is the performance level organization is looking forward from the job holder and the contribution of the job in the goal attainment of organization. The job related information is then used to create an organizational chart. It consists of different job classes, flow charts, flow of job activities and sharing points of different job profiles.

2. Selecting Representative Jobs for Analysis:

It is important to understand that analysis of jobs of organization is bit time consuming and costly affair. Thus, only some sample jobs are selected in order to carry out the detailed job analysis.

3. Collection of Data for Job Analysis:

The information related to different features of job and the abilities required to execute the job is collected from the organization. The job analysis tools such as observation, interviews, and questionnaire are used for the collection of data.

4. Preparing Job Description:

Based on the collected data the HR team prepares job description by defining the tasks, duties and responsibilities which are discharged for the effective performance.

5. Preparing Job Specification:

The job specification is prepared which consist of the personal traits, skills, qualities and qualification which are required to perform the job properly.

Job Analysis Methods & Techniques

Organizations have several methods and techniques to conduct the job analysis. Although the process of job analysis remains same, the methods used to collect the data differ from organization to organization. Here are some authentic methods to collect the data which is further used for job analysis-

1. Personal observation

In this method an observer is appointed by the organization to keep a watch on the individuals which performing the job. The observer then creates extensive list of task performed and the qualities of the individual which are utilized which executing the task. This method is useful but it does not work under certain condition. The task executed might be different every day and thus it is difficult to draw a conclusion based on few days of personal observation.

2. Actual execution of the job

The job analyzer can actually perform the job to get information about the skill requirement, difficulty while performing the job and efforts required to finish the given task.

3. Interview method

The information is collected about the job with the help of interviews of employees and their supervisors. The questions related to the skill level required, the task, the preparations needed to perform the job are asked during the interview. Although it is a time consuming technique it works well to gather information about the job. However many time both employee and supervisor forgets to mention certain aspects of the job. Many times the job responsibilities are exaggerated and thus make it difficult to define the job description and specification.

1. Questionnaires method

This is one of the least costly methods which can be used to collect data for job analysis. A well-designed and easy to understand questionnaires can be very useful to collect information regarding job in a short period of time. Multiple choice questions as well as open ended questions can be designed to understand the views of employees towards their job. The only drawback of this method is more number of incomplete forms and inaccurate information given by the employees about their job profile can lead into failure of job analysis.

2. Log records and HR records

The log record book created by the employee about their daily activities in the office is very useful type of job data. The records are extensive in nature and thus provide fair idea regarding the responsibilities and duties linked to the job. In a similar way the HR record can also be used as job data. It has information regarding the core competency of the employees, their experience history and promotions received. It also has employee's personal information such as educational qualification, previous job profile and job title and the year of experience.

3. Computerized Job Analysis

With the help of information communication technology, computerized job analysis systems are developed by researchers. Specificity of data is a significant attribute of computerized job Analysis. Job analysis database is created by compiling all the specific data together. It takes less effort and time to write job descriptions using computerized job analysis system. The job descriptions created using this method are quite accurate and linked with compensation system.

Apart from these methods few companies also use critical incident method in which the employee list out their experiences of critical incidents which performing the job. Combination methods are also used sometimes to get quick and accurate results.

Purpose or Objectives of Job Analysis

The purpose of job analysis is to do a detailed examination of employee job role, the working conditions of employees and the abilities and skill required to perform the job. The objectives of job analysis with respective HR activities is listed below-

- To determine efficient and effective method to execute a job
- To improve job satisfaction of employees
- To identify the needs of training and the core areas on which training should be given
- To develop a performance measurement system
- To match specification of employees with the job role they are offered during selection process.
- To provide standardized way to calculate the job compensation.

- To avoid ambiguity regarding the job duties and responsibilities of employee.

Benefits and Importance of Job Analysis

All most all the HR activities have greater use of job analysis. Here are some benefits and importance of job analysis from HR point of view-

1. Human Resource Planning:

Job analysis provides information such as how many employees which specific skill set is required to perform the job. This information is very necessary for human resource planning.

2. Recruitment and Selection:

A right person for right job is the objective of recruitment system. The job analysis provides information about the behavioral and personal attributes of the employees which can be utilized to make hiring process more effective.

3. Training and Development:

The information regarding the skills and knowledge required to perform a job is gathered through job analysis. Thus, based on job analysis organization can design relevant and appropriate <u>training and development</u> program for employees.

4. Placement and Orientation:

When HR department links the skill set of employees, with the job to be assigned it gets easier to make placement decision. The skill set required for a particular job is acquired through job analysis. It also provides information regarding the orientation required for new employee in order to perform well in the assigned job.

5. Job Evaluation:

The relative worth of a job and the appropriate salary structure of the job is determine in the job evaluation with the help of information provided by job analysis.

6. Performance Appraisal:

The job standards are established using job analysis. These job standards are utilize to rank the employees based on their performance and further carry out the performance appraisal process.

7. Personnel Information:

All the records of as Human Resource Information System (HRIS) are boasted using job analysis. It helps to improve the efficiency of administration and supports the decision making system of the organization.

8. Health and Safety:

Lastly the information regarding the working condition of a job is provided by job analysis. This information is used to create a safe and healthy work environment for the employees

methods of job analysis

Observation

In this method, the job analyst carefully observes the job holder at work and records what he or she does, how he or she does, and how much time is needed for completion of a given task. This method has both positive as well as negative sides. On the positive side, the method is simple, and the data collected are accurate because of direct observation. On the flip side, it may be told that the method is time consuming and inapplicable to jobs which involve high proportions of unobservable mental activities and those which do not have complete and easily observable job cycles.

The analyst needs to be trained to carefully observe and record the competence of a job incumbent. And training means additional cost. Considering all these, the observation method may be used for analyzing repetitive, short-cycle, unskilled and semi-skilled jobs. Better results will be available when the observation method is used along with other method(s) of job analysis.

Interview

In this, the analyst interviews the job holder and his/her supervisor to elicit information about the job. Usually, a structured interview form is used to record the information. During the interview, the analyst must make judgements about the information to be included and its degree of importance.

The interview method is time consuming. The time problem will be compounded if the interviewer talks with two or more employees doing the same job. Furthermore, professional and managerial jobs are more complicated to analyze and usually require a longer interview. Then, there ts the problem of bias. Bias on the part of the analyst and the job holder may cloud the accuracy and objectivity of the data obtained. The interview method has one positive feature, that is, it involves talking to the job holders who are in a good position to describe what they do, as well as the qualifications needed to perform their duties in a competent manner.

The effectiveness of the interview method depends on the interviewer and on the ability of the job holder to make meaningful responses.

Questionnaire

Job holders fill in the given structured questionnaires, which are then approved by their supervisors. The filled-in questionnaires offer enough data on jobs. Standard questionnaires are available or they may be prepared for the purpose by the analysts. Standard or prepared, questionnaires should contain the following basic information:

1. The job title of the job holder;

2. The job title of the job holder's manager or supervisor;

3. The job titles and numbers of the staff reporting to the job holder (best recorded by means of an organization chart);

4. A brief description (one or two sentences) of the overall role or purpose of the job; and

5. A list of the main tasks or duties that the job holder has to carry out; as appropriate, these should specify the resources controlled, the equipment used, the contracts made and the frequency with which the tasks are carried out.

The questionnaires method has its own advantages and limitations. The major advantage of the questionnaire method is that information on a large number of jobs can be collected in a relatively short period of time. But some follow-up observations and discussions are necessary to clarify inadequately filled-in questionnaires and interpretation problems. Further, the questionnaire method helps save time and the staff required to carry out the programme. Finally, all the job holders participate in the method unlike in an interview where one or two workers only would participate.

Checklists

A checklist is similar to a questionnaire, but the response sheet contains fewer subjective judgements and tends to be either-yes-or-no variety. Checklists can cover as many as 100 activities and job holders tick only those tasks that are included in their jobs. Preparation of a checklist is a challenging job. The specialists who prepare the list must collect all relevant information about the job concerned. Such information can be obtained by asking supervisors, industrial engineers, and others familiar with the work.

When a checklist has been prepared for a job, it is sent to the job holder. The job holder is asked to check all listed tasks that he/she performs and indicate the amount of time spent on each task as well as the training and experience required to be proficient in each task. He/she may also be asked to write any additional tasks he/she performs which is not stated in the checklist.

One advantage of the checklist method is that it is useful in large firms that have a large number of people assigned to one particular job. Also, this technique is amenable to tabulation and recording on electronic data-processing equipment. The technique, however, is costly and, hence, not suitable for small firms.

Technical Conference Method

In this method, services of supervisors who possess extensive knowledge about a job are used. It is from these experts that details about the job are obtained. Here, a conference of supervisors is used. The analyst initiates discussion which provides details about jobs. Though a good method of data collection, this method lacks accuracy because the actual job holders are not involved in collecting information.

Diary Method

This method requires the job holders to record in detail their activities each day. If done faithfully, this technique is accurate and eliminates errors caused by memory lapses the job holder makes while answering questionnaires and checklists. This method, however, is time consuming because the recording of tasks may have to be spread over a number of days. It also engages considerable time of a production worker. No wonder, the diary method is not used much in practice.

The methods described above are not to be viewed as mutually exclusive. None of them is universally superior. The best results can be obtained by a combination of these methods.

Quantitative Techniques

The methods of collecting job-related data, described above are used by most employers. But there are occasions where these narrative approaches are not appropriate. For example, where it is desired to assign a quantitative value to each job so that jobs can be compared for pay purposes, a more quantitative approach will be appropriate. The position analysis questionnaire, management position description questionnaire and functional job analysis are the three popular techniques of job analysis.

Position Analysis Questionnaire

The Position Analysis Questionnaire (PAQ) is a highly specialized instrument for analyzing any job in terms of employee activities. The PAQ contains 194 job elements on which a job is created depending on the degree to which an element (or descriptor) is present. These elements are grouped into six general categories.

The primary advantage of the PAQ is that it can be used to analyze almost every job. Further, this analysis provides a comparison of a specific job with other job classifications, particularly for selection and remuneration purposes. However, the PAQ needs to be completed by trained job analysts rather than incumbents or supervisors, since the language in the questionnaire is difficult and at a fairly high reading level.

Management Position Description Questionnaire

The Management Position Description Questionnaire (MPDQ) is a highly structured questionnaire containing 208 items relating to managerial responsibilities, restrictions, demands and other miscellaneous position characteristics.

Functional Job Analysis

Functional Job Analysis (FJA) is a worker-oriented job analytical approach which attempts to describe the whole person on the job. The main features of FJA include the following:

1. A fundamental distinction must be made between what has been done and what employees need to do to get the things done. For example, bus crew do not carry passengers, but they drive vehicle and collect fare.

2. Jobs are performed in relation to data, people and things.

3. In relation to things, employees draw on physical resources; in relation to data, employees draw on mental resources; and in relation to people, employees draw on

interpersonal resources.

4. All jobs require employees to relate data, people and things to some degree.

CHAPTER TWELVE

Uses of Job Analysis

Uses of Job Analysis

1. Human Resource Planning:
Job analysis is useful in human resource planning in terms of demand forecasting. It finds out the requisite knowledge and skills required to perform a job.

2. Recruitment:
Job analysis helps in recruitment in terms of finding how and when people should be hired for new job openings. It makes the recruitment process easier by highlighting the skills, knowledge and abilities required to perform a job.

3. Selection:
Job analysis helps in selecting the right person by making the employer understand what is to be done on a job.

4. Placement and Orientation:
Job analysis is useful in putting the newly selected person at the right place in the organization.

5. Training:
Job analysis eases the training process by identifying the duties and responsibilities associated with a job. If the

candidate doesn't have enough knowledge, then training is provided to make him effective.

6. Counselling:

Proper counselling of the employee is possible only after knowing the details about the employee's job. This helps in grooming the career of the employees.

7. Employee Safety:

Through a proper job analysis the analyst can know the health hazards and accidents associated with a job. By knowing, proper steps can be undertaken to eradicate those situations.

8. Performance Appraisal:

In case of performance appraisal the appraiser compares the performance of the employee with the standard performance based on job analysis. It makes the process of performance appraisal easy and simple.

9. Job Design and Redesign:

Through job analysis the details of job are identified. From this the weak areas in a job are identified. It helps in reducing unnecessary movements, simplify certain steps and improve the existing ones through continuous monitoring.

10. Job Evaluation:

It is finding the relative worth of a job in relation to other jobs in the organization. This is done with the help of the job analysis. Job evaluation helps in fixing the pay package of employees with internal and external pay equity.

Problems with Job Analysis

No process can be entirely accurate and fully serves the purpose. Job analysis is no exception to it. The process involves a variety of methods, tools, plans and a lot of human effort. And where 'people' are involved, nothing can be 100 percent accurate. However, they may be appropriate considering various factors including organizational requirements, time, effort and financial resources. Since the entire job analysis processes, methods and tools are designed by humans only, they tend to have practical issues associated with them. Human brain suffers with some limitations, therefore, everything created, designed or developed by humans too have some or other constraints.

Coming back to the subject, even the process of job analysis has lot of practical problems associated with it. Though the process can be effective, appropriate, practical, efficient and focused but it can be costly, time consuming and disruptive for employees at the same time. It is because there are some typical problems that are encountered by a job analyst while carrying out the process. Let's discuss them and understand how the process of job analysis can be made more effective by treating them carefully.

Problems with Job Analysis

- **Lack of Management Support:** The biggest problem arises when a job analyst does not get proper support from the management. The top management needs to communicate it to the middle level managers and employees to enhance the output or productivity of the process. In case of improper communication, employees may take it in a wrong sense and start looking out for other available options. They may have a notion that this is being carried out to fire them or take any action against them. In order to avoid such circumstances, top management must effectively communicate the right message to their incumbents.

- **Lack of Co-operation from Employees:** If we talk about collecting authentic and accurate job-data, it is almost impossible to get real and genuine data without the support of employees. If they are not ready to co-operate, it is a sheer wastage of time, money and human effort to conduct job analysis process. The need is to take the workers in confidence and communicating that it is being done to solve their problems only.

- **Inability to Identify the Need of Job Analysis:** If the objectives and needs of job analysis process are not properly identified, the whole exercise of investigation and carrying out research is futile. Managers must decide in advance why this process is being carried out, what its objectives are and what is to be done with the collected and recorded data.

- **Biasness of Job Analyst:** A balanced and unbiased approach is a necessity while carrying out the process of job analysis. To get real and genuine data, a job analyst must be impartial in his or her approach. If it can't be avoided, it is better to outsource the process or hire a professional job analyst.

- **Using Single Data Source:** A job analyst needs to consider more than one sources of data in order to collect true information. Collecting data from a single source may result in inaccuracy and it therefore, defeats the whole purpose of conducting the job analysis process.

However, this is not the end. There may be many other problems involved in a job analysis process such as insufficient time and resources, distortion from incumbent, lack of proper communication, improper questionnaires and other forms, absence of verification and review of job analysis process and lack of reward or recognition for providing genuine and quality information.

Advantages and Disadvantages of Job Analysis

Though job analysis plays a vital role in all other human related activities but every process that has human interventions also suffers from some limitations. The process of job analysis also has its own constraints. So, let us discuss the advantages and disadvantages of job analysis process at length.

Advantages of Job Analysis

- **Provides First Hand Job-Related Information:** The job analysis process provides with valuable job-related data that helps managers and job analyst the duties and responsibilities of a particular job, risks and hazards involved in it, skills and abilities required to perform the job and other related info.
- **Helps in Creating Right Job-Employee Fit:** This is one of the most crucial management activities. Filling the right person in a right job vacancy is a test of skills, understanding and competencies of HR managers. Job Analysis helps them understand what type of employee will be suitable to deliver a specific job successfully.
- **Helps in Establishing Effective Hiring Practices:** Who is to be filled where and when? Who to target and how for a specific job opening? Job analysis process gives answers to all these questions and helps managers in creating, establishing and maintaining effective hiring practices.

- **Guides through Performance Evaluation and Appraisal Processes:** Job Analysis helps managers evaluating the performance of employees by comparing the standard or desired output with delivered or actual output. On these bases, they appraise their performances. The process helps in deciding whom to promote and when. It also guides managers in understanding the skill gaps so that right person can be fit at that particular place in order to get desired output.
- **Helps in Analyzing Training & Development Needs:** The process of job analysis gives answer to following questions:

  - Who to impart training
  - When to impart training
  - What should be the content of training
  - What should be the type of training: behavioral or technical
  - Who will conduct training

- **Helps in Deciding Compensation Package for a Specific Job:** A genuine and unbiased process of job analysis helps managers in determining the appropriate compensation package and benefits and allowances for a particular job. This is done on the basis of responsibilities and hazards involved in a job.

Disadvantages of Job Analysis

- **Time Consuming:** The biggest disadvantage of Job Analysis process is that it is very time consuming. It is a major limitation especially when jobs change frequently.

- **Involves Personal Biasness:** If the observer or job analyst is an employee of the same organization, the process may involve his or her personal likes and dislikes. This is a major hindrance in collecting genuine and accurate data.

- **Source of Data is Extremely Small:** Because of small sample size, the source of collecting data is extremely small. Therefore, information collected from few individuals needs to be standardized.

- **Involves Lots of Human Efforts:** The process involves lots of human efforts. As every job carries different information and there is no set pattern, customized information is to be collected for different jobs. The process needs to be conducted separately for collecting and recording job-related data.

- **Job Analyst May Not Possess Appropriate Skills:** If job analyst is not aware of the objective of job analysis process or does not possess appropriate skills to conduct the process, it is a sheer wastage of company's resources. He or she needs to be trained in order to get authentic data.

- **Mental Abilities Can not be Directly Observed:** Last but not the least, mental abilities such as intellect, emotional characteristics, knowledge, aptitude, psychic and endurance are intangible things that can not be observed or measured directly. People act differently in different situations. Therefore, general standards can not be set for mental abilities.

CHAPTER THIRTEEN

Recruitment

Recruitment means announcing job opportunities to the public and stimulating them in such a way so that a good number of suitable people will apply for them. Recruitment is the process of discovering the potential for actual or anticipated organizational vacancies.

It is a process of accumulation of human resources for the vacant positions of the organization.

Recruitment refers to the process of attracting, screening, and selecting qualified people for a job at an organization or firm.

Recruitment is a continuous process whereby the firm attempts to develop a pool of qualified applicants for future human resources needs even though specific vacancies do not exist.

Usually, the recruitment process starts when a manager initiates an employee requisition for a specific vacancy or an anticipated vacancy.

Meaning of Recruitment

Successful human resource planning should identify human resource needs. Once these needs are identified, HR managers can do something to meet them.

A company's growth is measured according to its profits and losses. The cost of unnecessary hiring and/or hiring the wrong person can be detrimental to a company's bottom line.

Before engaging in the <u>recruitment process</u>, management should clearly understand the company's operational requirements, projected revenues, and business goals and then determine the types of skills and competencies required to meet those needs.

Successful human resource planning should identify human resource needs, as mentioned earlier.

The next step is the acquisition function of human resource management. Recruitment is the first stage of the acquisition function.

According to Keith Davis, "Recruitment is the process of finding and attracting capable applicants for employment. The process begins when recruits are sought and ends when their applications are submitted."

According to Edwin B. Flippo, "Recruitment is the process of searching for prospective employees and stimulating them to apply for jobs in the organization."

Recruitment Functions

Recruitment is the process by which companies find and hire new employees.

The HR department is usually responsible for recruitment. This department works to find and attract capable applicants. Job descriptions and specifications provide the needed information upon which the recruitment process rests,

The HR manager who recruits and initially screens for the vacant job is seldom responsible for supervising its performance.

So he needs the help of line HR. Both line and HR staff work together.

recruitment forces

The recruitment function of the organizations is direct or indirect ways affected by a mix of various internal and external forces.

The internal forces or the factors that can be controlled by the organization and the external factors are those factors which cannot be controlled by the organization.

The internal and external <u>forces affecting recruitment function</u> of an firm are:

INTERNAL FACTORS

The internal factors likewise term as endogenous elements are the components inside the association that impact selecting in the organisation

The internal forces i.e. the factors which can be controlled by the organization are:

1. Recruitment Policy

The <u>recruitment policy of the organization</u> i.e. recruiting from internal sources and external also affect the recruitment process. The recruitment policy of an organization determines the destinations or enlistment and gives a structure to usage of recruitment program.

Factors Affecting Recruitment Policy

- Need of the organization.
- Organizational objectives
- Preferred sources of recruitment.
- Government policies on reservations.
- Personnel policies of the organization and its competitors.
- Recruitment costs and financial implications.

2. Human Resource Planning

Effective human resource process and procedure helps in fixing the loops present in the existing manpower of the organization. This also helps in filter the number of employees to be recruited and what kind qualification and skills they must possess.

3. Size of the Organization

The size of the organization affects the recruitment process. If the organization is planning to increase its operations and expand its business, it will think of hiring more personnel, which will handle its operations.

4. Cost involved in recruitment

Recruitment process also count the cost to the employer, thats why organizations try to employ/outsource the

<u>source of recruitment</u> which will be cost effective to the organization for each candidate.

5. Growth and Expansion

Organization will utilize or consider utilizing more work force in the event that it is growing its operations.

EXTERNAL FACTORS

The external forces are the forces which cannot be controlled by the organization. The major external forces are:

1. Supply and Demand

The availability of manpower both within and outside the organization is an essential factor in the recruitment process.

2. Labour Market

Employment conditions where the organization is located will effected by the recruiting efforts of the organization.

3. Goodwill / Image of the organization

Image of the firm is another factor having its effect on the Different government controls forbidding separation in contracting and work have coordinate effect on enlistment practices. As taken Example, Govt. of India has the convention of reservation in work for booked standings/ planned clans, physically Disabled and so on. Additionally, exchange associations have the significant part in enrollment. This limits management freedom to select those individuals who can be the best performers.This can work as a potential constraint for recruitment. A company with positive image as an employer able to easier to attract and retain employees than an organization with negative image. Organisations actions and activities like good public relations, public service like,charity, contruction and developement roads, public parks, hospitals education and schools help earn image or goodwill for organization.

4. Political-Social- Legal Environment

Different government controls forbidding separation in contracting and work have coordinate effect on enlistment practices.

5. Unemployment Rate

The Element that influence the availability of applicants is the economy growth rate . At the point when the organization isn't making new jobs, there is frequently oversupply of qualified work which thusly prompts unemployment.

6. Competitors

The recruitment policies and procedure an of the competitors also affect the recruitment function of the organizations.Time to time the organizations have to change their recruitment policies and manuals according to the policies being followed by the competitors.

Recruitment is one of the main departments which place the right candidates to the right job. The recruiters should identify the best candidates from different sources and job sites. Recruiters have to identify the problems faced during recruitment and find an alternative to make work efficiently which can fulfil recruitment goal on time .

Objectives of Recruitment Policy

Recruitment policy asserts the recruitment objectives and provides a framework for the implementation of the recruitment program.

It may involve the organization system to be developed for implementing recruitment programs and procedures to be employed.

According to Memoria, a good recruitment policy must contain elements such as

1. the organization's objective (short term and long term),
2. identification of the recruitment needs,
3. the preferred source of recruitment,
4. criteria of selection and preferences, and
5. the cost of recruitment and its financial implications of the same. Objectives are targets and goals.

According to Yoder (1996), the following are the main objectives of recruitment policy:

- To find and employ the best-qualified person for each job.

- To minimize the cost of recruitment.
- To offer promising careers and security.
- To provide facilities for growth and development.
- To retain the best and most promising ones.
- To reduce the scope of favoritism and malpractice.

HR Challenges in Recruitment

Recruitment is a function that requires business perspective, expertise, ability to find and match the best potential candidate for the organization, diplomacy, marketing skills (as to sell the position to the candidate), and wisdom to align the recruitment processes for the benefit of the organization.

The HR professionals – handling the organization's recruitment function- are constantly facing new challenges in Recruitment. The biggest HR challenge in Recruitment for such professionals is to source or recruit the best people or potential candidates for the organization.

In the last few years, the job market has undergone some fundamental changes in terms of technologies, recruitment sources, competition in the market, etc.

In an already saturated job market, where practices like poaching and raiding are gaining momentum. HR professionals are constantly facing new challenges in one of their most important functions- recruitment.

They have to face and conquer various challenges to find the best candidates for their organizations.

The major challenges faced by HR in recruitment are:

Adaptability to globalization

The HR professionals are expected and required to keep in tune with the changing times, i.e., the changes taking place across the globe. HR should maintain the timeliness of the process.

Lack of motivation

Recruitment is considered to be a thankless job. Even if the organization is achieving results, the HR department or professionals are not thanked for recruiting the right employees and performers.

Process analysis

The immediacy and speed of the recruitment process are the main concerns of HR in recruitment. The process should be flexible, adaptive, and responsive to the immediate requirements.

The recruitment process should also be cost-effective.

Strategic prioritization

The emerging new systems are both an opportunity as well as a challenge for the HR professionals.

Therefore, reviewing staffing needs and prioritizing the tasks to meet the changes in the market has become a challenge for recruitment professionals.

Technological changes

The decision to strategy development relates to the methods used in recruitment and selection. The available technology mainly influences this decision. The advent of computers has made it possible for employers to scan national and international applicant qualifications.

Although impersonal, computers have given employers and job seekers a wider scope of options in the internal screening' stage.

Technological advancement has made it possible for job seekers to gain better access. They have begun sending C.V. about themselves to some organizations without wasting time and without spending money on travel.

Sources of recruitment

Two types of sources of recruitment are available such as;

- internal sources (present employees, employee referrals, former employees, and previous applicants), and
- external sources (trade associations, advertisements, employment exchanges, campus recruitment, walk-ins and write-ins, consultants, radio and television, competitors and E-recruiting, etc.).

Competition in the market

Rival firms can be a source of recruitment. Popularly called poaching or raiding, this method involves identifying the right people in the rival companies, offering them better terms, and luring them away. To reduce costs, organizations look into labor markets likely to offer the required job seekers.

Generally, companies look into the national market for managerial and professional employees, regional or local markets for technical employees, and local markets for clerical and blue-collar employees.

Sources of Recruitment

There are basically two sources of supply from where potential employees can be drawn. These are internal sources and external sources. Internal sources indicate recruiting qualified people from within the organization itself (from the present working force).

When reference is made to the number of employees already employed by the organization, we speak of the internal supply.

Whenever any vacancy occurs, someone from within the organization is upgraded, promoted, or transferred to another department also goes into the category of an internal source of recruitment.

External recruitment is concerned with generating a pool of qualified candidates through external sources of employment.

The external sources of recruitment include – employment at the factory gate, advertisements, employment exchanges, employment agencies, educational institutes, labor contractors, recommendations, etc.

Advantages and disadvantages are associated with promoting from within the organization and hiring outside the organization to fill openings.

Advantages of internal recruiting

- The people responsible for selecting internal candidates for vacant positions have access to more comprehensive information about their abilities, track record, and potential achievement than they would have if selecting people originating from an external source.

- It is motivating to employees, as they are preferred over outsiders when the vacancies occur. Employees tend to be committed to firms under the circumstances.
- It provides an opportunity for advancement.
- It is economical in terms of time and money.
- It improves employee morale.
- It improves the image of the organization.
- It improves the probability of better performance as the candidate is in a better position to know the objectives and expectations of the organization.

The demerits of the internal source

- The promotion may be biased in nature and may be based on seniority rather than merit.
- Possible moral problems emerged for those who have not been promoted.
- Political infighting for promotions.
- An option may be limited in locating the right talents.
- This channel of recruitment discourages new blood from entering the organization.
- Inhibits innovation and creativity.
- Establishes subjectivity in the promotion.

Promotion from within should be aided by __careful employee selection__. The employment process should favor those applicants who have the potentials for promotion.

Effective promotion from within also depends on other HR actions. It depends on providing the education and training needed to help employees identify and develop their promotion potential. It also requires a career-oriented appraisal.

Advantages of external sources

Recruiting from outside the organization is known as an external source.

All firms more or less rely on external sources. Advantages of external sources are: o It offers the organization the opportunity to inject new ideas into its operations by utilizing the skills of external candidates.

- Improves the knowledge and skill of the organization by recruiting from outside sources.
- Improves and helps in sustaining competitive advantage.
- Brings the economy in the long run.

Disadvantages of external sources

- It is costly.
- It causes brain drain due to fear of lack of growth potential.
- It contributes to a higher probability of employee turnover.
- Demoralization of existing employee for alleged double standard and favor shown towards new recruitment from outside by offering better position and pay.

Purpose and Importance of Recruitment

The Purpose and Importance of Recruitment are given below:

- Attract and encourage more and more candidates to apply to the organization.
- Create a talent pool of candidates to enable the selection of the best candidates for the organization.
- Determine present and future requirements of the organization in conjunction with its personnel planning and **job analysis activities**.
- Recruitment is the process that links the employers with the employees.
- Increase the pool of job candidates at minimum cost.
- Help increase the success rate of the selection process by decreasing the number of visibly underqualified or overqualified job applicants.
- Help reduce the probability that job applicants, once recruited and selected, will leave the organization only after a short period of time.
- Meet the organization's legal and social obligations regarding the composition of its workforce.
- Begin identifying and preparing potential job applicants who will be appropriate candidates.
- Increase organization and individual effectiveness of various recruiting techniques and sources for all types of job applicants.

CHAPTER FIFTEEN

Methods of recruiting

The HR department can use different methods for recruiting. These are as follows:

Walks-ins and write-ins

Walk-ins are job seekers who arrive at the HR department in search of a job.

Write-ins are those who send a written inquiry. Both groups are asked to complete an application blank to determine their interests and abilities.

Employee referrals

Employees may refer job seekers to the HR department.

Advertising

It is the most widely used method as it can reach a wider candidate pool. It describes the jobs and the benefits, identifies the employer, and tells those who are interested in how to apply.

It is the most widely used method as it can reach a wider candidate pool. It describes the jobs and the benefits, identifies the employer, and tells those who are interested in how to apply.

Various media are used for advertisement such as newspapers, journals, TV, Radio, etc. Proper design of the advertisement will have the following merits:

- Encourage the right persons to apply.
- Discourage unsuitable persons from applying.

However, the advertisement copy must contain such information as

- <u>Job description</u>,
- Job specification,
- Job pricing,

Blind advertisement is another technique used by some organizations. The blind and does not identify the employer.

Interested applicants are told to send their resumes to a mailbox number at the post office or newspaper. Reputed and well-known organization seldom uses blind advertisement.

Blind ads have some severe limitations such as:

- They may lead to thousands of job seekers for one job opening.
- Many suitable candidates may not apply because they feel that the company may have a poor reputation in withholding their identification.
- Many consider such advertisement as regularization action in which recruitment has already been made.
- Very few may apply for less attractive jobs.

State employment agencies

Every government has a state employment agency. It is designed to help job seekers to find suitable employment. This agency matches job seekers with job openings.

When an employer has a job opening, the HR department voluntarily notifies the employment service of the job and its requirements.

Private placement agencies

Private employment agencies developed in the vacuum created by the poor image of the public employment service.

They do charge fees either from a potential employee, employers, or both for their services. Placement firms take an employer's request for recruits and then solicit job seekers, usually through advertising or among walk-ins.

Candidates are matched with the employer's request and then told to <u>report to the employer's HR department for an interview</u>.

Some of the agencies become specialized in certain categories of employment like the following:

- Security guards,
- Clerical or computer operators
- Engineers
- Pharmacists
- Bankers
- Salesmen
- Accountants

Recruitment Process: 4 Steps of Recruiting Best Talents

1. Identifying the HR Requirement

The first step of recruitment is to assess the <u>requirement of human resources in an organization</u> to carry out the organizational mission, goals, and objectives.

Under this step, the required number and kinds of people needed for organizational performance are identified. It can be done through the information obtained from HR planning and <u>job analysis</u>.

This provides information on the current availability of human resources and anticipates the future requirement of HR for organizational activities.

Under it, a comprehensive draft is prepared to specify the duties, responsibilities, working conditions, and skill requirements to perform the task.

2. Identifying possible sources of HR Supply

After assessing HR requirements, the probable sources are identified for generating a pool of qualified candidates. This process involves searching for potential candidates.

Mainly sources of HR supply are of two types: internal sources and external sources. Internal sources consist of <u>transfers</u> and <u>promotions</u>, whereas external sources include various alternatives like employment agencies, advertisements, casual callers, recommendations, educational institutions, etc.

Along with the probable sources, a suitable recruitment method is also identified under this phase of recruitment. The sources and methods are adopted in such a way that they provide the best and qualified human resources at a minimum cost.

3. Communicating the Information

In this step of recruitment, the potential candidates are informed about the vacancy announcement.

Under it, the information about the job requirement is passed away to the potential candidates about the job and required several employees to be recruited.

This information is passed away through different media or from the organization's notice board. The popular media for vacancy announcements are print media, electronic media, the internet, etc.

4. Receiving Application

The recruitment process ends by generating a pool of qualified candidates to fill organizational vacancies. Under it, a recruiter receives the application forms dropped by different applicants interested in applying for a job. It provides a pool of candidates for selection.

After recruitment, the <u>selection process</u> begins, which chooses the best applicant for the job who is supposed to perform well in the actual work situation.

After receiving application forms, they are evaluated to check whether the basic requirement is maintained or not.

Conclusion

Recruitment is a process to discover the workforce sources to meet the recruitments of the staffing schedule and employ effective measures for attracting human resources in adequate numbers to facilitate the effective selection of an efficient working force.

Selection

Selection is the process of choosing the most suitable candidates from those who apply for the job. It is a process of offering jobs to desired candidates.

Once the potential applicants are identified, the next step is to evaluate their qualification, qualities, experience, capabilities, etc. & make the selection. It is the process of offering jobs to the desired applicants.

Selection means choosing a few from those who apply. It is picking up of applicants or candidates with requisite qualifications and qualities to fill jobs in the organization.

Definition of Selection

According to Harold Koontz, "Selection is the process of choosing from the candidates, from within the organization or from outside, the most suitable person for the current position or for the future positions."

Dale Yoder said, "Selection is the process by which candidates for employment are divided into classes those who will be offered employment and those who will not."

Selection is the process of choosing from a group of applicants those individuals best suited for a particular position.

Most managers recognize that employee selection is one of their most difficult, and most important, business decisions.

This process involves making a judgment -not about the applicant, but about the fit between the applicant and the job by considering knowledge, skills and abilities and other characteristics required to perform the job Selection procedures are not carried out through standard pattern and steps in this.

The process can vary from organization to organization some steps performed and considered important by one organization can be skipped by other organization.

Personnel Selection is the methodical placement of individuals into jobs. Its impact on the organization is realized when employees achieve years or decades of service to the employer.

The process of selection follows a methodology to collect information about an individual in order to determine if that individual should be employed. The methodology used should not violate any laws regarding personnel selection.

Steps in Selection Process

The selection process typically begins with the preliminary interview; next, candidates complete the application for employment.

They progress through a series of selection tests, the employment interview, and reference and background checks. The successful applicant receives a company physical examination and is employed if the results are satisfactory.

Several external and internal factors impact the selection process, and the manager must take them into account in making selection decisions.

Typically selection process consists of the following steps but it is not necessary that all organization go through all these steps as per the requirement of the organization some steps can be skipped while performing the selection process.

. *Initial Screening*

The selection process often begins with an initial screening of applicants to remove individuals who obviously do not meet the position requirements.

At this stage, a few straight forward questions are asked. An applicant may obviously be unqualified to fill the advertised position, but be well qualified to work in other open positions.

The Purpose of Screening is to decrease the number of applicants being considered for selection.

Sources utilized in the screening effort

Personal Resume presented with the job application is considered a source of information that can be used for the initial screening process. It mainly includes information in the following areas:

- Employment & education history.
- Evaluation of character.
- Evaluation of job performance.

Advantages of Successful Screening

If the screening effort is successful, those applicants that do not meet the minimum required qualifications will not move to the next stage in the selection process. Companies utilizing expensive selection procedures put more effort into screening to reduce costs.

2. Completion of the Application Form

Application Blank is a formal record of an individual's application for employment. The next step in the selection process may involve having the prospective employee complete an application for employment.

This may be as brief as requiring only an applicant's name, address, and telephone number. In general terms, the application form gives a job-performance-related synopsis of applicants' life, skills and accomplishments.

The specific type of information may vary from firm to firm and even by job type within an organization. Application forms are a good way to quickly collect verifiable and fairly accurate historical data from the candidate.

3. Employment Tests

Personnel testing is a valuable way to measure individual characteristics.

Hundreds of tests have been developed to measure various dimensions of behavior. The tests measure mental abilities, knowledge, physical abilities, personality, interest, temperament, and other attitudes and behaviors.

Evidence suggests that the use of tests is becoming more prevalent for assessing an applicant's qualifications and potential for success. Tests are used more in the public sector than in the private sector and in medium-sized and large companies than in small companies.

Large organizations are likely to have trained specialists to run their testing programs.

Advantages of using tests

Selection testing can be a reliable and accurate means of selecting qualified candidates from a pool of applicants.

As with all selection procedures, it is important to identify the essential functions of each job and determine the skills needed to perform them.

Potential Problems using Selection tests

Selection tests may accurately predict an applicant's ability to perform the job, but they are less successful in indicating the extent to which the individual will want to perform it.

Another potential problem, related primarily to personality tests and interest inventories, has to do with applicants honesty. Also, there is the problem of test anxiety.

Applicants often become quite anxious when confronting yet another hurdle that might eliminate them from consideration.

4. Job Interview

An interview is a goal-oriented conversation in which the interviewer and applicant exchange information. The employment interview is especially significant because the applicants who reach this stage are considered to be the most promising candidates.

Interview Planning

Interview planning is essential to effective employment interviews.

The physical location of the interview should be both pleasant and private, providing for a minimum of interruptions. The interviewer should possess a pleasant personality, empathy and the ability to listen and communicate effectively.

He or she should become familiar with the applicant's qualifications by reviewing the data collected from other selection tools. In preparing for the interview, a job profile should be developed based on the job description.

Content of the Interview

The specific content of employment interviews varies greatly by an organization and the level of the job concerned.

1. **Occupational experience:** Exploring an individual's occupational experience requires determining the applicant's skills, abilities, and willingness to handle responsibility.
2. **Academic achievement:** In the absence of significant work experience, a person's academic background takes on greater importance.
3. **Interpersonal skills:** If an individual cannot work well with other employees, chances for success are slim. This is especially true in today's world with increasing emphasis being placed on the use of teams.
4. **Personal qualities:** Personal qualities normally observed during the interview include physical appearance, speaking ability, vocabulary, poise, adaptability, and assertiveness.
5. **Organizational fit:** A hiring criterion that is not prominently mentioned in the literature is organizational fit. Organizational fit is ill-defined but refers to management's perception of the degree to which the prospective employee will fit in with, for example, the firm's culture or value system.

5. Conditional Job Offer

Conditional job offer means a tentative job offer that becomes permanent after certain conditions are met.

If a job applicant has passed each step of the selection process so far, a conditional job offer is usually made.

In essence, the conditional job offer implies that if everything checks out – such as passing a certain medical, physical or substance abuse test – the conditional nature of the job offer will be removed and the offer will be permanent.

6. Background Investigation

Background Investigation is intended to verify that information on the application form is correct and accurate.

This step is used to check the accuracy of application form through former employers and references. Verification of education and legal status to work, credit history and criminal record are also made.

Personal reference checks may provide additional insight into the information furnished by the applicant and allow verification of its accuracy.

Past behavior is the best predictor of future behavior. It is important to gain as much information as possible about past behavior to understand what kinds of behavior one can expect in the future.

Knowledge about attendance problems, insubordination issues, theft, or other behavioral problems can certainly help one avoid hiring someone who is likely to repeat those behaviors.

Background investigations primarily seek data from references supplied by the applicant including his or her previous employers. The intensity of background investigations depends on the level of responsibility inherent in the position to be filled.

Common sources of background information include:

- References are provided by the applicant and are usually very positive.
- Former employers should be called to confirm the candidate's work record and to obtain their performance appraisal.
- Educational accomplishments can be verified by asking for transcripts.
- Legal status to work.
- Credit references, if job-related.
- Criminal records can be checked by third-party investigators.
- Background checks are conducted by third-party investigators.
- Online searches as simple as "Google" search of a candidate can turn up information on press releases or news items about a candidate that was left off the application or resume.

7. Medical/Physical Examination

After the decision has been made to extend a job offer, the next phase of the selection process involves the completion of a medical/physical examination.

This is an examination to determine an applicant's physical fitness for essential job performance.

Typically, a job offer is contingent on successfully passing this examination.

For example, firefighters must perform activities that require a certain physical condition. Whether it is climbing a ladder, lugging a water-filled four-inch hose or carrying an injured victim, these individuals must demonstrate that they are fit for the job.

8. Permanent Job Offer

Individuals who perform successfully in the preceding steps are now considered eligible to receive the employment offer. The actual hiring decision should be made by the manager in the department where the vacancy exists.

Where Recruitment Ends Selection Starts

Recruitment involves attracting and obtaining as many applications as possible from eligible job seekers. Recruitment is the process of finding and attracting capable applicants for employment.

The process begins when new recruits are sought and ends when their applications are submitted. The result is a pool of applicants from which new employees are selected.

Selection is the process of differentiating between applicants in order to identify and hire those with a greater likelihood of success in a job. Though some selection methods can be used within the organization for promotion or transfer, in this case, the statement of the question is not correct.

But when the selection of applicants from outside the organization has occurred then the given statement in the question is correct.

Recruitment and relation are the two crucial steps in the HR process and are often used interchangeably. There is however a fine distinction between the two steps.

While recruitment refers to the process of identifying and encouraging prospective employees to apply for jobs, the selection is concerned with picking the right candidates from the pool of applicants which are obtained during the recruitment process.

So in this case selection is derived from after completing the <u>recruitment process</u>. Recruitment is said to be positive in its approach as it seeks to attract as many candidates as possible.

Selection, on the other hand, is negative in its application in as much as it seeks to element as many unqualified applicants as possible in order to identify the right candidates from the pool.

So in the recruitment and selection process; <u>recruitment is the first step</u> and selection is the second steps or final step.

In conclusion, we can say "When recruitment ends selection to start.

Conclusion

The objectives of the selection process are to select the candidates whose success probability in the job is the highest and motivate right candidates to opt for the vacancy by a proper presentation of the organization to the potential candidates.

In many HR departments, recruiting and selection are combined and called the employment function. In large HR departments, the employment function is the responsibility of the HR Director.

In smaller departments, HR managers handle these duties.

The selection process relies on three helpful inputs. Job analysis information provides the description of the jobs, the human specifications and the performance standards each job requires.

Human resource plans tell HR managers what job openings are likely to occur. These plans allow selection to proceed in a logical manner.

Finally, recruits are necessary so that the HR manager has a group of people from which to choose. These three inputs largely determine the effectiveness of the selection process.

The selection process is a series of steps through which applicants pass.

For example, a candidate who fails to qualify for a particular step is not eligible for appearing for the subsequent step. The result of each step is crucial. Failure of any step disqualifies the candidate from attempting the next step.

Because of this characteristic, Yoder (1972) has termed this process as a succession of hurdles. It is designed to determine the most likely candidates to be successful at fulfilling the job requirements by eliminating those candidates least likely to succeed.

job evaluation

A **job evaluation** is a systematic way of determining the value/worth of a job in relation to other jobs in an organization. It tries to make a systematic comparison between jobs to assess their relative worth for the purpose of establishing a rational pay structure. Job evaluation needs to be differentiated from job analysis. Job analysis is a systematic way of gathering information about a job. Every job evaluation method requires at least some basic job analysis in order to provide factual information about the jobs concerned. Thus, job evaluation begins with job analysis and ends at that point where the worth of a job is ascertained for achieving pay equity between jobs and different roles.

Process

The process of job evaluation involves the following steps:

- **Gaining acceptance:** Before undertaking job evaluation, top management must explain the aims and uses of the program to managers, emphasizing the benefits. Employees and unions may be consulted, depending on the legal and employee relations environment and company culture. To elaborate the program further, presentations could be made to explain the inputs, processes, and outputs/benefits of job evaluation.

- **Creating job evaluation committee**: It is not possible for a single person to evaluate all the key jobs in an organization. Often a job evaluation committee consisting of experienced employees, union representatives, and HR experts is created to set the ball rolling.
- **Finding the jobs to be evaluated**: Every job need not be evaluated. This may be too taxing and costly. Certain key jobs in each department may be identified. While picking up the jobs, care must be taken to ensure that they represent the type of work performed in that department, at various levels.
- **Analysing and preparing job description**: This requires the preparation of a job description and also an analysis of job specifications for successful performance. See job analysis.
- **Selecting the method of evaluation**: The method of evaluating jobs must be identified, keeping the job factors as well as organizational demands in mind. Selecting a method also involves consideration of company culture and the capacity of the compensation and benefits function or job evaluation committee.
- **Evaluating jobs**: The relative worth of various jobs in an organization may be determined by applying the job evaluation method. The method may consider the "whole job" by ranking a set of jobs, or by comparing each job to a general level description. Factor-based methods require consideration of the level of various compensable factors (criteria) such as level and breadth of responsibility, knowledge, and skill required,

complexity, impact, accountability, working conditions, etc. These factor comparisons can be one with or without numerical scoring. If there is numerical scoring, weights can be assigned to each such factor and scores are associated with different levels of each factor, so that a total score is determined for the job. All methods result in an assigned grade level.

Methods

There are primarily three methods of job evaluation: (1) ranking, (2) classification, (3) Factor comparison method or Point method. While many variations of these methods exist in practice, the three basic approaches are described here.

Ranking method

Perhaps the simplest method of job evaluation is the ranking method. According to this method, jobs are arranged from highest to lowest, in order of their value or merit to the organization. Jobs can also be arranged according to the relative difficulty in performing them. The jobs are examined as a whole rather than on the basis of important factors in the job; the job at the top of the list has the highest value and obviously the job at the bottom of the list will have the lowest value. Jobs are usually ranked in each department and then the department rankings are combined to develop an organizational ranking. The variation in payment of salaries depends on the variation of the nature of the job performed by the employees. The ranking method is simple to understand and practice and it is best suited for a small organization. Its simplicity however works to its disadvantage in big organizations because rankings are difficult to develop in a large, complex organization. Moreover, this kind of ranking is highly subjective in nature and may offend many employees. Therefore, a more scientific and fruitful way of job evaluation is called for.

Classification method (Grading method)

According to this method, a predetermined number of job groups or job classes are established and jobs are assigned to these classifications. This method places groups of jobs into job classes or job grades. Separate classes may include office, clerical, managerial, personnel, etc. Following is a brief description of such a classification in an office.

- Class I - Executives: Further classification under this category may be Office Manager, Deputy office manager, Office superintendent, Departmental supervisor, etc.
- Class II - Skilled workers: Under this category may come the Purchasing assistant, Cashier, Receipts clerk, etc.
- Class III - Semiskilled workers: Under this category may come Stenotypists, Machine-operators, Switchboard operator etc.
- Class IV - Unskilled workers: This category may comprise peons, messengers, housekeeping staff, Daftaris[clarification needed], File clerks, Office boys, etc.

The job grading method is less subjective when compared to the earlier ranking method. The system is very easy to understand and acceptable to almost all employees without hesitation. One strong point in favour of the method is that it takes into account all the factors that a job comprises. This system can be effectively used for a variety of jobs. The weaknesses of the Grading method are:

- Even when the requirements of different jobs differ, they may be combined into a single category, depending on the status a job carries.
- It is difficult to write all-inclusive descriptions of a grade.
- The method oversimplifies sharp differences between different jobs and different grades.
- When individual job descriptions and grade descriptions do not match well, the evaluators have the tendency to classify the job using their subjective judgements.

Factor comparison method or Point method

This method is widely used and is considered to be one of the reliable and systematic approach for job evaluation in mid and large size organisations. Most consulting firms adopt this method, which was pioneered by Edward Hay in 1943. Here, jobs are expressed in terms of key factors. Points are assigned to each factor after prioritizing each factor in order of importance. The points are summed up to determine the wage rate for the job. Jobs with similar point totals are placed in similar pay grades. The procedure involved may be explained thus:

1. Select key jobs. Identify the factors common to all the identified jobs such as skill, effort, responsibility, etc.

2. Divide each major factor into a number of sub factors. Each sub factor is defined and expressed clearly in the order of importance, preferably along a scale.

The most frequent factors employed in point systems are:

(i) Skill (key factor); Education and training required, Breadth/depth of experience required, Social skills required, Problem-solving skills, Degree of discretion/use of judgment, Creative thinking

(ii) Responsibility/Accountability: Breadth of responsibility, Specialized responsibility, Complexity of the work, Degree of freedom to act, Number and nature of subordinate staff, Extent of accountability for equipment/plant, Extent of accountability for product/materials;

(iii) Effort: Mental demands of a job, Physical demands of a job, Degree of potential stress

The educational requirements (sub factor) under the skill (key factor) may be expressed thus in the order of importance.

3. Find the maximum number of points assigned to each job (after adding up the point values of all sub-factors of such a job).

This would help in finding the relative worth of a job. For instance, the maximum points assigned to an officer's job in a bank come to 540. The manager's job, after adding up key factors + sub factors points, may be getting a point value of say 650 from the job evaluation committee. This job is now priced at a higher level.

4. Once the worth of a job in terms of total points is expressed, the points are converted into money values keeping in view the hourly/daily wage rates. A wage survey is usually undertaken to collect wage rates of certain key jobs in the organization.

Merits and demerits

The point method is a superior and widely used method of evaluating jobs. It forces raters to look into all key factors and sub-factors of a job. Point values are assigned to all factors in a systematic way, eliminating bias at every stage. It is reliable because raters using similar criteria would get more or less similar answers. The methodology underlying the approach contributes to a minimum of rating error (Robbins p. 361). It accounts for differences in wage rates for various jobs on the strength of job factors. Jobs may change over time, but the rating scales established under the point method remain unaffected. On the negative side, the point method is complex. Preparing a manual for various jobs, fixing values for key and sub-factors, establishing wage rates for different grades, etc., is a time-consuming process, According to Decenzo and Robbins, "the key criteria must be carefully and clearly identified, degrees of factors have to be agreed upon in terms that mean the same to all rates, the weight of each criterion has to be established and point values must be assigned to degrees". This may be too taxing, especially while evaluating managerial jobs where the nature of work (varied, complex, novel) is such that it cannot be expressed in quantifiable numbers.

Limitations

1. Job evaluation is not completely scientific.
2. Different job evaluators may reach different results, requiring validation

3. More complex systems, such as point factor, may be difficult to explain to managers or employees

Concept of job evaluation

What is job design? As we just explained, job analysis provides job-related data as well as the skills and knowledge required for the <u>incumbent</u> to perform the job. A better job performance also requires deciding on sequence of job contents. This is called '<u>job design</u>'. Job design is a logical sequence to job analysis. In other words, job design involves specifying the contents of a job, the work methods used in its performance and how the job relates to other jobs in the organisation.

A few definitions on job design are produced here with a view to help you understand the meaning of job design in a better manner. Michael Armstrong[11] has defined job design as "the process of deciding on the contents of a job in terms of its duties and responsibilities, on the methods to be used in carrying out the job, in terms of techniques, systems and procedures, and on the relationships that should exist between the job holder and his superiors, subordinates and colleagues".

Mathis and Jackson[12] have defined job design as "a process that integrates work content (tasks, functions, relationships), the rewards(extrinsic and intrinsic), and the qualifications required (skills, knowledge, abilities) for each job in a way that meets the needs of employees and organisations."

Popplewell and Wildsmith[13] define job design in these words: ".......involves conscious efforts to organise tasks, duties, and responsibilities into a unit of work to achieve certain objectives".

Having gone through the above definitions of job design, it can now be described as a deliberate attempt made to structure both technical and social aspects of the job to attain a fit between the individual (job holder) and the job. The very idea is that job should be designed in such a way as to enable employees to control over the aspects of their work. The underlying justification being that by doing this, it enhances the quality of the work life, harnesses the potential of the workers in a more effective manner and thereby improves employee performance.

CHAPTER EIGHTEEN

Employee retention

Employee retention is a phenomenon where employees choose to stay on with their current company and don't actively seek other job prospects. The opposite of retention is turnover, where employees leave the company for a variety of reasons.

Retention is defined as the process by which a company ensures that its employees don't quit their jobs. Every company and industry has a varying retention rate, which indicates the percentage of employees who remained with the organization during a fixed period.

Let's look at the different types of turnover and how they impact your retention rate with a few examples.

Example 1 Imagine a scenario where an employee has been working at your company for over five years. Their spouse is forced to relocate to a different city for medical reasons. In this case, retaining the employee may be next to impossible, especially if it is an on-premise job.

Example 2 Now, consider an employee who joined your company a couple of years ago and grew quickly through the ranks. But lately, the employee has become complacent as the job is no longer challenging for them. They become a passive job seeker and might be scooped up by a recruiter from a different company. By keeping your eye on the employees engagement level, it is possible to retain them.

Different Employee Retention Strategies

Every company strives to hold onto its people assets for the longest time. This improves productivity, maintains uninterrupted business flows, and reduces the cost of rehiring. That is why retention is a top priority for most organizations. But in a competitive hiring climate, employee retention can often be a challenge.

By applying the right tactics, you can hold onto your best-performing talent and create a workforce thats loyal, engaged, and outcome-focused. Its important to remember that retention strategies will differ from employee to employee.

So, what are the different strategies you can deploy to ensure maximum retention? Keep in mind that your high-performing talent isnt likely to have the same drivers as the mid-performing group. Similarly, poor performers need different retention strategies altogether.

Retention strategies for top performers

Did you know that, according to McKinsey, high performers are likely to be 400% more productive than their average-performing counterparts? While this number may vary from company to company, its definitely worth paying special attention to retention strategies for this group.

Give them challenging work

By continually giving your top performers a new target to work toward, you can keep them engaged. This strategy also helps them further their careers, allowing them to acquire new skills and achievements. The positive impact on their overall employability will make top performers more loyal to your company.

2. Train them in cross-disciplinary skills

Once an employee becomes an expert in one area, you can open them up to cross-skilling opportunities. This will ensure that the employee doesn't jump ship in search of their "dream job" and has a chance to transition to a similar role within the company laterally.

3. Define and implement a succession plan

Succession planning creates a <u>talent pipeline</u>, preparing todays top performers for future leadership roles. Involving this employee group in your succession plan can be a good idea for retention, as they know exactly where they are headed in the company.

Retention strategies for average performers

Average performers form the majority of the workforce in most companies. As a result, they are also responsible for a large portion of your productivity. For example, if you run a car showroom, the average salespeople will bring in at least 50% of total sales, while the top-performing group could be bringing in another 40%. Thats why retention strategies for this segment are equally important. Note that these strategies can be added to those for high performers.

Offer personalized benefits and perks

Personalized benefits can be an excellent way of retaining your employees, as it gives them a sense of security about their future and a better quality of life. Conduct surveys to find out the most popular benefits and double down on your investments in these areas.

2. Ensure they are working under the right manager

Inadequate management will make employees feel demotivated, or even disgruntled with their job. This is particularly relevant for average performers, as they often lack the quality of self-motivation that characterizes high-performing employees. Conduct anonymized pulse surveys to get employee feedback on their managers.

3. Adopt a social recognition system to recognize them

The contributions of average-performing employees shouldnt be ignored. By adopting a social reward and recognition platform, you can make them feel appreciated in the workplace and thereby less likely to quit.

Retention strategies for poor performers

Low-performing employees might have hidden potential that is not being utilized correctly. They could be working in the wrong department, while their aptitude lies elsewhere. Or they simply might require additional training. A wave of turnover among poor performers can negatively impact your culture, not to mention lead to high rehiring costs. To avoid this, you should consider the following steps.

Identify the cause of poor performance

In several cases, below-average performance can be linked to disengagement in the workplace. You must find these patterns and address them before it is too late. Measure productivity at regular intervals and deploy an <u>employee engagement survey</u>whenever you find productivity dipping below a specific threshold.

2. Address skill gaps immediately

By offering your poor performers the chance to update their skill set, you can make sure they stay on in the company for a longer time. The fact that the company is invested in their performance is likely to increase their loyalty to the organization. However, also ensure that these employees are trainable. Even a basic level of training should be able to add to their overall performance in the organization.

3. Write accurate job descriptions to hire the right people

Some employees will join your company with wholly different expectations from what the job really entails. For example, a software developer might want to create products but in reality, they will end up writing code for someone elses design and feature ideas. Make these details explicit in your job description, as well during onboarding to prevent a dip in performance, leading to a turnover.

Training and Development

Training and Development is one of the most important functions of **Human Resource management** in any of the organization. The objective of this Training is to enhance employees' skills behavior and expertise by putting them into learning new techniques of doing work.

Employee Training and Development helps in updating employees' skills and knowledge for performing a Job which at the end results in increasing their work efficiency and increase the productivity of an organization. It ensures that Employees oddness or eccentricity is reduced and learning or behavioral change should take place in a very structured format. Training development or learning and development are official ongoing educational activities designed for goal fulfillment and enhance the performance of employees.

The activities linked with employee Training & Development is created to convey the employee to perform better in assigned job which also motivate employee to give his/her best so that at the time of <u>performance appraisal</u>, employee can show the eligibility for <u>promotion</u> and <u>salary increment</u>. It refers as the skill and knowledge enhancing bustle which is a source of additional information as well as instruction required to improve the quality of performance. HR Training and Development are two different activities which goes hand-in-hand for the overall betterment of the employee. The short term and reactive process is training which is used for operational purpose while the long term process of development is for executive purpose. The aim of training in HRM is to improvement of required skills in the employee whereas aim of development is to improve overall personality of the employee. Management takes the initiative of training to fill up the skill gap in the organization; the development initiative is generally taken with the objective of future succession planning.

Definition:

Employee Training and Development in HRM is defined as a system used by an organization to improve the skills and performance of the employees. It is an educational tool which consists of information and instructions to make existing skills sharp, introduce new concepts and knowledge to improve the employee performance. An effective training & development initiative based on <u>training needs analysis</u>helps the company to enhance the skills of working manpower and improve productivity.

Meaning:

A program of upgrading of employee's skills, knowledge and competencies is known as training. The job related training is often provided to the employee to ensure they can well perform on the assigned tasks and contribute to the success of the organization. The development program on the other hand is often preparation to perform the future job. Human Resource Training Development provides a learning opportunity to the employee to increase their work capacities and get ready for the future challenges.

Training and development in HRM are two different activities which goes hand-in-hand for the overall betterment of the employee. The short term and reactive process is training which is used for operational purpose while the long term process of development is for executive purpose. The aim of training & development is improvement of required skills in the employee whereas aim of development is to improve overall personality of the employee. Management takes the initiative to choose right **training methods** to fill up the skill gap in the organization; the development initiative is generally taken with the objective of future succession planning.

Training and Development Definition by the Eminent Authors

Here below are the definitions given by the expert and eminent authors:

Armstrong

"Training is the formal and systematic modification of behavior through learning which occurs as a result of education, instruction, development and planned experience. Development is improving individual performance in their present Roles and preparing them for greater responsibilities in the future".

Katz & Kahn

"Training and development is described as a maintenance subsystem, intended to improve organizational efficiency by increasing routinization and predictability of behavior".

Training and Development in Human Resource Management (HRM)

Training and development is always identified as one of the vital <u>Human Resource</u> functions. In most of the organizations training and development is an integral part of the HRD (human resource development) activity. Among the cut-throat competition in the corporate world where skilled manpower is important aspect to gain competitive advantage, training & development acts as a tool for success of organization. As rapid changes in technology are deskilling the employees very quickly, many organizations have fixed certain amount of training hours per year for their employees.

The HRD department is focused towards the improvement of the manpower of the organization. The training and development activities are often used to motivate employees and improve their organizational commitment. The HR department has found out that employee really appreciate that they have given an opportunity to build new skills and improve their <u>job performance</u>. Employee feels that organization is totally commitment towards the growth of their manpower and thus they like to be a part of training and development activities. The training development activities are also used to attract new talent towards the organization by publicizing the HRD efforts.

From the HR perspective, training and development activities are best way to create talent pool in the organization. Instead of hiring staff which is skilled and trained for a particular job profile, training and development activities running in the organization is much cheaper source of internal skilled employees. It reduces the **recruitment** or hiring cost of the organization and due to internal hiring for particular position the employee joining on new post is already aware of the organizational work culture. HRD department also promotes HR training and development activities as the homegrown executives are found to perform better than skilled people hired from outside.

HRD department is usually in-charge of planning and execution of training & development activities in the organization. This activity includes first search of skill gaps in the organization and then finding a right source from which the employees can learn new skills and improve their performance. It is well said that through training and development activity the **HRM** department actually contribute to the productivity of the organization.

Need of Training and Development

- The training and development activity is required when company revises its objectives and goal to adjust the changing market conditions.
- Companies often endorse training and development programs to improve the performance of the employees.
- The HR training and development is needed to set up a benchmark of performance which employees are expected to achieve in a financial year.
- There is always a need of training and development efforts to teach the employee new skills such as team management, communication management and leadership behavior.

- Training and development is also used to test new methods of enhancing organizational productivity.

CHAPTER NINETEEN

Importance of training and development in an organization

New Hire Orientation

Training is particularly important for new employees. This can be conducted by someone within the company and should serve as a platform to get new employees up to speed with the processes of the company and address any skill gaps.

Tackle shortcomings

Every individual has some shortcomings and training and development helps employees iron them out. For example, at RateGain we have divided the entire headcount in several groups to provide focused training which is relevant to those groups - sales training, first time managers, middle management, senior leadership, executive leadership.

Improvement in performance

If shortcomings and weaknesses are addressed, it is obvious that an employee's performance improves. Training and development, however, also goes on to amplify your strengths and acquire new skill sets. It is important for a company to break down the training and development needs to target relevant individuals. If I can draw examples from my organization, every department has targeted training groups. These generally revolve around product development training, QA training, PMP among others where internal and external process experts facilitate various programs.

Employee satisfaction

A company that invests in training and development generally tends to have satisfied employees. However, the exercise has to be relevant to the employees and one from which they can learn and take back something. It will be futile if training and development become tedious and dull, and employees attend it merely because they have to. As a company, we stress on industry specific training and send many employees for international seminars and conferences that can be beneficial to them.

Increased productivity

In a rapidly evolving landscape, productivity is not only dependent on employees, but also on the technology they use. Training and development goes a long way in getting employees up to date with new technology, use existing ones better and then discard the outdated ones. This goes a long way in getting things done efficiently and in the most productive way.

Self driven

Employees who have attended the right trainings need lesser supervision and guidance. Training develops necessary skill sets in employees and enable them to address tasks independently. This also allows supervisors and management to focus on more pressing areas.

To transform our company into a learning organization and encourage a culture of continual learning among employees, we have launched a training and development initiative called 'RateGain Lighthouse'. We call it lighthouse, as it symbolizes strength, guidance and direction. We conduct various in-house training sessions on knowledge-building and skills & process.

The network facilitates various training sessions, based on experiential learning methodologies. We have also engaged globally renowned experts like Aaron Ross, author of 'Predictable revenue' and world renowned Sales coach and trainer. His session for our sales teams have transformed the way we are working. The results from our training and development initiatives have been very positive and it clearly shows that it is not a fad.

Training and development programs can have a huge impact on a company. Like every other function in your company, training and development should be focused on producing targeted and tangible results for the business. The key is to treat it seriously and consider it a capital investment and make it results-driven.

Training and Development Programmes

Training and development programmes are designed according to the requirements of the organisation, the type and skills of employees being trained, the end goals of the training and the job profile of the employees. These programmes are generally classified into two types: (i) on the job programmes, and (ii)off the job programmes.

Different training is given to employees at different levels. The following training methods are used For the training of skilled workers and operators- Specific job training programmes, Technical training at a training with live demos, Internship training, Training via the process of rotation of job.

Training given to people in a supervisory or managerial capacity is – Lectures, Group Discussions, Case studies, Role-playing, Conferences etc.

People in managerial programmes are given this type of training- Management Games to develop decision making, Programmes to identify potential executives, Sensitivity training to understand and influence employee behaviour, Simulation and role-playing, Programmes for improving communication, human relations and managerial skills.

Other Training Programmes

Technical Training – Technical training is that type of training that is aimed at teaching employees how a particular technology or a machine.

Quality Training – Quality training is usually performed in companies who physically produce a product. Quality training teaches employees to identify faulty products and only allow perfect products to go out to the markets.

Skills Training – Skills training refers to training given to employees so as to perform their particular jobs. For e.g. A receptionist would be specifically taught to answer calls and handle the answering machine.

Soft Skills – Soft skills training includes personality development, being welcoming and friendly to clients, building rapport, training on sexual harassment etc.

Professional Training – Professional Training is done for jobs that have constantly changing and evolving work like the field of medicine and research. People working in these sectors have to be regularly updated on matters of the industry.

Team Training – Team training establishes a level of trust and synchronicity between team members for increased efficiency.

Benefits of Training

1. Training improves the quantity and quality of the workforce. It increases the skills and knowledge base of the employees.
2. It improves upon the time and money required to reach the company's goals. For e.g. Trained salesmen achieve and exceed their targets faster than inexperienced and untrained salesmen.
3. Training helps to identify the highly skilled and talented employees and the company can give them jobs of higher responsibilities.
4. Trained employees are highly efficient in comparison to untrained ones.
5. Reduces the need to constantly supervise and overlook the employees.
6. Improves job satisfaction and thus boosts morale.

Benefits of Development

1. Exposes executives to the latest techniques and trends in their professional fields.

2. Ensures that the company has an adequate number of managers with knowledge and skill at any given point.
3. Helps in the long-term growth and survival of the company.
4. Creates an effective team of managers who can handle the company issues without fail.
5. Ensures that the employees utilise their managerial and leadership skills in particular to the fullest.

The Most Effective Training Methods

Research on training methods is essential to avoid the unnecessary costs that come with training. According to *Forbes*, the training market is worth approximately $109 billion in the United States. Therefore, the tasks of researchers are to search and define the best methods to present the information to the targeted trainees, as well as to find the right approach to investing in project management training.

One excellent study that explores such training methods is "Training Methods: A Review and Analysis." The authors of this article performed an integrative review of some of the most popular training methods. In addition to defining the core methods for training, the study does the following:

- Defines the key characteristics of the chosen types of training methods
- Researches the conditions in which the training methods are most suitable

1. Case Study

The case study is a proven method for training and is known to effectively boost learner motivation. However, when learners lack access to the resources necessary to completing a case study or if the project become a challenge, their motivation and learning will be hindered.

This method is suitable for situations when the trainees have the core knowledge but can still benefit from training. Because this method comes with lower costs, it's also one of the more popular methods in different disciplines like law, counseling, and medicine.

2. Games-Based Training

Games have been used for many educational purposes, including training. Using games for education is affordable, competitive, and motivational, especially in the digital era, in which many applicants and employees are highly involved with technology.

One of the disadvantages of this method is the inability to determine the components in a game that will contribute to the training itself. Trainers can't really make sure that every learning concept will be accepted by the trainees through game playing.

Still, game-based training teaches students to compete in environments like business, sports, or law.

3. Internship

Internships are great for both sides. Employers can benefit from the help of employees, while employees can benefit from the guidance of and training by employers. Still, in some cases, this can be high-pressured or inconsistent.

However, in situations and environments where the learners have some base knowledge and the employers are supportive and understanding, this is an excellent training method.

4. Job Rotation

Job rotation can do a lot in terms of employee motivation and commitment. This method gives people chances to further develop and work toward a promotion and engenders satisfaction and cooperation. Still, for introverts, this is often a big challenge because of the fear that they might fail in front of others. Also, it's a method that requires a lot of time and room for error.

But with the right background knowledge, both of these problems can be eliminated or at least reduced.

5. Job Shadowing

Job shadowing serves to generate employees' engagement and interest. Trainees get a chance to see their work from another perspective, which is perfect for those who are being considered for a promotion or a role change.

6. Lecture

Lectures are often dreaded and ridiculed, but they are the most commonly used training techniques. Yes, there is often a lack of interaction, but with the right speaker and simple lectures, this can lead to optimal learning.

7. Mentoring and Apprenticeship

When companies plan to groom people for promotion and growth, this is the best training method to use. Trainees can truly benefit from such a personalized learning structure, boost the mentor-trainee relationship, and facilitate their future career.

8. Programmed Instruction

Programmed instruction doesn't work without self-discipline, so it is most effective in cases when some straying from the program isn't detrimental to the company's success. Even so, this is an effective and flexible practice.

9. Role- Modeling

This is the counterpart of the lecture training method—one that promotes practice on lifelike models. It's often used in cases when employees need some practice after they see a lecture or a demonstration.

10. Role-Play

With role-playing, trainees can practice what they've learned in a personalized and simulated situation. They can still fail, but with good content and safe role-playing, there won't be any serious consequences.

11. Simulation

Simulation becomes more affordable every day. As such, it's commonly used for training that is considered costly or dangerous if performed in a real environment. This is a safe way to practice what would otherwise be risky.

12. Stimulus-Based Training

Stimulus-based training is a bit unconventional, but it's becoming more popular as time passes. It's a widely applied method that might make trainees a bit uncomfortable but can also enable them to acquire thorough knowledge faster than the other methods of training described here.

13. Team Training

Team training has a big and important goal: to connect a team. As such, it doesn't focus on trainees as individuals like the previously discussed methods; rather, this method is used to connect team members and make them more engaged in their training and work.

Kirkpatrick's Four-Level Training Evaluation Model

Understanding Kirkpatrick's Four Levels

Donald Kirkpatrick, former Professor Emeritus at the University of Wisconsin, first published his model in 1959. He updated it in 1975, and again in 1993, when he published his best-known work, "Evaluating Training Programs."

Each successive level of the model represents a more precise measure of the effectiveness of a training program. It was developed further by Donald and his son, James; and then by James and his wife, Wendy Kayser Kirkpatrick.

In 2016, James and Wendy revised and clarified the original theory, and introduced the "New World Kirkpatrick Model" in their book, "<u>Four Levels of Training Evaluation</u>." One of the main additions is an emphasis on the importance of making training relevant to people's everyday jobs.

The four levels are **Reaction**, **Learning**, **Behavior**, and **Results**. We look at each level in greater detail, and explore how to apply it, below.

Level 1: Reaction

You want people to feel that training is valuable. Measuring how engaged they were, how actively they contributed, and how they reacted to the training helps you to understand how well they received it.

It also enables you to make improvements to future programs, by identifying important topics that might have been missing.

Questions to ask trainees include:

- Did you feel that the training was worth your time?
- Did you think that it was successful?
- What were the biggest strengths and weaknesses of the training?
- Did you like the venue and presentation style?
- Did the training session accommodate your personal <u>learning styles</u> ?
- Were the training activities engaging?
- What are the three most important things that you learned from this training?

- From what you learned, what do you plan to apply in your job?
- What support might you need to apply what you learned?

Identify how you want to measure people's reactions. Many people use <u>employee satisfaction surveys</u> to do this, but you can also watch trainees' <u>body language</u> during the session, or ask for verbal feedback.

Analyze the feedback, and consider the changes that you could make in response.

Level 2: Learning

Level 2 focuses on measuring what your trainees have and haven't learned. In the New World version of the tool, Level 2 also measures what they think they'll be able to do differently as a result, how confident they are that they can do it, and how motivated they are to make changes.

This demonstrates how training has developed their skills, attitudes and knowledge, as well as their confidence and commitment.

To measure how much your trainees have learned, start by identifying what you want to evaluate. Training sessions should have specific <u>learning objectives</u> , so make those your starting point.

You can measure learning in different ways, depending on the objectives. But it's helpful to measure these areas both before and after training.

Before the training begins, test your trainees to determine their knowledge, skill levels and attitudes. Then, when the training is finished, test your trainees a second time to measure what they have learned, or measure their learning with interviews or verbal assessments.

Note:

As a manager, you need to <u>hold people accountable</u> for improving their skills, and to offer them the support they need to do so.

Level 3: Behavior

This level helps you to understand how well people apply their training. It can also reveal where people might need help. But behavior can only change when conditions are favorable.

Imagine that you're assessing your team members after a training session. You can see little change, and you conclude that they learned nothing, and that the training was ineffective.

It's possible, however, that they actually learned a lot, but that the organizational or team culture obstructs behavioral change. Perhaps existing processes mean that there's little scope to apply new thinking, for example.

As a result, your people don't feel confident in applying new knowledge, or see few opportunities to do so. Or, they may not have had enough time to put it into practice.

Be sure to develop processes that encourage, reinforce and reward positive changes in behavior. The New World Kirkpatrick Model calls these processes "required drivers." If a team member uses a new skill effectively, highlight this and praise him or her for it.

Effectively measuring behavior is a longer-term process that should take place over weeks or months following the initial training. Questions to ask include:

- Did the trainees put any of their learning to use?

- Are trainees able to teach their new knowledge, skills or attitudes to other people?
- Are trainees aware that they've changed their behavior?

One of the best ways to measure behavior is to conduct observations and interviews. Another is to integrate the use of new skills into the tasks that you set your team, so that people have the chance to demonstrate what they know.

Tip:

Managers need to be closely involved at this stage, assessing and **coaching** their team members in making behavior changes.

Level 4: Results

At this level, you analyze the final results of your training. This includes outcomes that you or your organization have decided are good for business and good for your team members, and which demonstrate a good return on investment (ROI). (Some adapted versions of the model actually have a Level 5, dedicated to working out ROI.)

Level 4 will likely be the most costly and time-consuming. Your biggest challenge will be to identify which outcomes, benefits, or final results are most closely linked to the training, and to come up with an effective way to measure these outcomes in the long term.

Modern trainers often **use the Kirkpatrick model backward**, by first stating the results that they want to see, and then developing the training that is most likely to deliver them. This helps to prioritize the goals of the training and make it more effective.

Here are some outcomes to consider, depending on the objectives of your training:

- Increased employee retention.
- Increased production.
- Higher morale.
- Reduced waste.
- Increased sales.
- Higher quality ratings.
- Increased customer satisfaction.
- Fewer staff complaints.

Make a series of short-term observations and measurements to check that changes in behavior due to training are making a worthwhile difference to your team's performance. The New World Kirkpatrick Model calls these "leading indicators."

impediments to effective training

An effective training program will reap huge benefits. Alternatively, improper training can be counterproductive to the organizational goals. There are several reasons why trainings often fail in companies, regardless of the size of the organization.

Avoiding common barriers to effective organizational learning & training can take you a long way in redefining the success of your training efforts and in making the most out of your investment.

But what is it that prevents employees from learning at work? Let's take a closer look at some of the biggest barriers to organizational learning and how to overcome each barrier.

What are the Barriers to Learning in an Organization?

The following are the most common barriers to Organizational learning & training program:

1. Program Focus vs Organizational Focus

2. Limited Resources
3. Resistance to Change
4. Work-Learning Dichotomy
5. Lack of Leadership
6. Non-Learning Culture
7. Short-Term Focus

1. Program FocusvsOrganizational Focus

Typically, your employees' attention is on the program or project delivery, not on organizational improvement. Employees put their energy and time into delivering assigned projects and programs.

Program focus is one of the most significant barriers to Organizational learning. Making your employees complete the task effectively and compelling them to do what is been assigned will make no improvements.

How to overcome Program focus barriers to the training program?

Explaining to your employees the following factors is one of the best ways to overcome **Program focus** barrier to Organizational learning:

- Why do they need to do this?
- What's in it for them?
- Is there any alternative way of doing it?
- What skills they can acquire?

2. *Limited Resources*

When the economic downturn hits, many organizations chop their training and development budgets. Companies must see training as an **"investment."**

Most individuals love the feeling of learning something new. Limited resource is one of the barriers for Organizational learning. The management must create resources for those who are fond of studying – especially in the workplace.

How to overcome limited resource barriers to Organisational learning?

<u>Research from ClearCompany</u> suggests that more than 68% of employees say Training & Development is the company's most important policy. This shows the employees value learning to a great extent.

Create your organizational structures such as Policies, Standards, Regulations, Budget, and expenses such that they motivate your employees to learn and improve themselves rather than forbidding them to do so.

Try to implement creative & effective ways to build learning into the day-to-day activities of the organization.

3. Resistance to Change

Employee resistance to change is a significant barrier to Organizational learning. Individuals who are accustomed to a particular way of functioning over a long period, tend to avoid doing something new. They don't want to learn or change to new processes.

It is common for some employees to feel like they might lose familiarity that they have with existing systems & processes.

For an organization to evolve, it is necessary to change. Change initiatives help you to adapt to the current market trends, internal processes, the latest technological advancements, and more.

How to overcome employee resistance to Training Programs & Organisational learning?

To prevent employee resistance, you must explain to your employees why the change is essential and also why now? You can highlight the benefits and try to implement some wow factors in there to gain their trust.

If you want to learn more strategies for dealing with employee change resistance, here's just the guide for you, best practices and effective solution to <u>overcome change resistance</u>.

4. Work-Learning Dichotomy

In many organizations, work and learning are considered as two different aspects of employment, and work, invariably, always has the highest priority. A work learning culture means that the company's values support learning in a meaningful & effective way.

Another big barrier to organizational learning in the workplace is your employee frustration in trying to improve their skills and knowledge without any support from the organization.

How to overcome this common barrier to Organisational learning?

Make sure you provide learning opportunities to your employees and motivate them to learn new things and grow themselves. Organizations can emphasize learning in their communication about organizational values & goals.

Boost your employees' learning culture. Make sure your employees don't complain saying that they don't have time to complete their learning & training. Research more about organizational <u>learning & development</u> and invest in effective training tools if needed.

5.Lack ofLeadership

For any organization to continue to learn & adapt, leadership must be engaged in their key processes of learning & performance improvement.

Many leaders avoid confrontation, tough questions & awkward discussions. Improper leadership leads to chaos and acts as a massive barrier to <u>Organizational learning & training</u> programs.

How to overcome a lack of leadership acting as a barrier to Organisational learning?

Organizational learning must be prioritized in a top-down manner and bucketed into different stages, with leaders involved at each stage. Leaders must be well equipped to boost employee confidence and morale.

6. Non-Learning Culture

Non-learning culture prevents your employees from wanting to learn something new. In an organization where learning is not encouraged or promoted, it is difficult for employees to make the most of their trainings.

Organizations can provide a learning environment but must be aware of various problems that will arise and end up as barriers to organizational learning.

How to overcome non-learning culture as a barrier to Organisational learning?

Identify the pain points of your employees and address them as early as possible. Provide value and opportunities for learning in the workplace. Showcase the benefits of learning and you can recognize the fast learners to motivate others.

7.Short-TermFocus

Temporary solutions and short-term vision are barriers to Organizational learning. Leaders usually tend to gravitate towards the most obvious problem without considering all the future consequences.

How to overcome Short-term focus barriers to Organizational learning?

Organizational learning is an on-going process and so it adds up when you focus on the big picture rather than short-term goals. Encourage your leaders to allocate time for deciding long-term vision and provide <u>employee learning opportunities</u> all the time.

Organizational learning might involve complex content. Complexity can overwhelm your employees and act as a barrier to training in the workplace. The long-term focus must consider all these complexities and provide an easy & effective way of learning to your employees.

CHAPTER TWENTY

Performance appraisal

Performance appraisal is defined as a process that systematically measures an employees personality and performance usually by managers or immediate supervisors against the predefined attributes like skillset, knowledge about the role, technical know-how, attitude, punctuality and so on.

Performance appraisal has many names across organizations, some call it performance evaluation, some prefer performance review, merit rating, annual reviews, etc.

This process is carried out to identify the inherent qualities of an employee and the abilities and level of competency of an employee for their future growth and development and that of the organization they are associated with. It aims at ascertaining the value of an employee and his/her offering to the organization.

Performance appraisal helps managers and supervisors place the right employee to do the right job, depending on the skill set they possess. Without an ounce of doubt, every organization needs a robust performance appraisal system.

There are various methods that are used by managers and supervisors to evaluate employees based on objective and subjective factors, however, it can get a bit tricky, but to effectively evaluate an employee both factors are essential.

Objectives of performance appraisal

Following are the objectives to conduct performance appraisal year after year:

- This is an essential first step towards promoting an employee, based on the subjective and objective factors-performance and competency.
- To identify the training and development needs of an employee.
- To provide confirmation to those employees who were recently hired and are on their probation period.
- To take a concrete decision what should be the percentage of hike in the salary of an employee based on the work done by them.
- To encourage a proper feedback system between the manager and employees.
- To help employees understand where they stand in the current year and what is the scope of improvement.

1. Provide Feedback:

Appraisals are an effective way to give feedback to employees Also, managers to communicate clearly regarding employee objectives and expectations. An employee can learn about what he/she can do to improve their future performance.

In addition, Some tips for employee feedback

1. Performance Outcome

2. Quarterly Reviews

3. Give feedback on a 1-2-1 basis

2. Downsize or Right-Size:

The COVID pandemic is one of the many harsh realities that might force an organization to downsize. In such a situation, appraisals are a way to make sure that the most productive and talented individuals can be retained in a company. It is also an effective way to know which employees are non-performers.

3. Promote The Right Person:

Appraisals give an organization objective and data-driven tools to make good promotion decisions Also, It helps the most talented individuals retain the position of the highest importance.

4. Set Goals & Measure Goals:

The annual appraisals are also an effective way to set future goals for the employees. This ensures maximum productivity and superior performance.

5. Improve Work Performance:

An employee can only improve if he knows how to Objectives of a good appraisal include highlighting the specific area of improvement for every employee.

Some tips improve performance:

1. Keep your eyes on the deadline
2. Also, Improve project evaluation skills
3. Set Goals as well as Personal Benchmarks

6. Determine Compensation Changes:

An appraisal system works as a determining factor in increasing compensation, pay raises, etc. Also, It ensures that people who work harder get paid better.

7. Encourage Coaching & Mentoring:

Managers are usually expected to coach their team members Also, appraisals help the managers to identify the areas where mentoring is required.

8. Employee Training and Development:

Individual skills are evaluated during an appraisal. Also, this helps employees to identify if they need to acquire more skills and competencies to contribute to the company. It also helps an organization to plan the up-skilling training for their employees.

9. Provide a Legal Defense For Personal Decisions:

A company can be held accountable for any decision that they take, even firing or promoting an employee. Therefore, conducting a performance appraisal will help the company prove a point if their decisions are ever challenged.

10. Encouraging Coaching & Mentoring:

Teaching and coaching are part of managing employees. It is part of being a good manager. Performance appraisals will help them understand where an employee is lacking therefore where they can train and help employees to do better.

11. Improving Overall Organization's Performance:

Last but not least, performance appraisals will help the company to learn more about the employees and their requirements. It will help the employees to understand where they are lacking and where they are doing well. This will help them learn and grow quickly.

Performance appraisal process

Step 1: In most organizations, the performance appraisal process means evaluating an employee every 6 months or one year for the period an employee has continually worked with the organization. In modern times, the Human Resources department sends out an employee survey for them to fill out to collect data related to their engagement and satisfaction levels.

Step 2: The employee's immediate manager or supervisor will then evaluate the quality of the employee's performance based on the work done in the previous year and then meet face-to-face to discuss the facts and figures.

Step 3: The feedback received from the survey can be kept anonymous. This feedback can be analyzed real-time by using QuestionPro's Workforce platform, that measures, analyzes and activates data to get actionable insights.

For probationary employees, the probation period usually lasts between three to six months. Their evaluation is based on whether they have come at pace with the work and culture of the organization and if they are ready to take up more responsibilities.

Performance appraisal methods

There are 5 performance appraisal methods. Using one of these methods for performance appraisal can help organizations gain partial information. However, combining one or more methods will lead to extracting better information and accurate data. It is one thing to collect data and another to do something actionable with it.

1. **Self-evaluation:** This is an important way to get insights from the employees, evaluate themselves. You need to first get information about how an employee evaluates himself/herself, after conducting this evaluation the management has an opportunity to fairly appraise an employee based on their thoughts.
2. **360-degree appraisal system:**360-degree feedback, an employee is evaluated by his/her supervisor/manager,

peers, colleagues, subordinates and even management. Inputs from different sources are considered before talking to the employee face-to-face. In this process, each employee is rated according to the job done based on the job descriptions assigned to them.

3. **Graphics rating scale:** This is one of the most commonly used methods by managers and supervisors. Numeric or text values corresponding to values from excellent to poor can be used on this scale. Members of the same team who have similar job descriptions can be parallelly evaluated using this method. This scale should ideally be the same for each employee.

4. **Checklists:** The evaluator is given a checklist of several behaviors, traits, attributes or job description of the employee who needs to be evaluated. The checklist can contain sentences or simply attributes and the evaluator thus marks the employee based on what describes the job performance of the employee. If the evaluator believes that the employee has certain traits it is marked positive otherwise it is left blank.

5. **Essay method:** This is also known as "free form method". As the name suggests, it is a descriptive method which elaborates performance criteria. A major drawback of this method is to keep biases away.

Advantages of performance appraisal

1. A systematic performance appraisal method helps the managers/supervisors to correctly identify the performance of employees and also highlight the areas they need improvement in.
2. It helps the management place the right employee for the right kind of job. This is a win-win situation for both

the employee and the organization.

3. Potential employees who have done some exceptional work are often offered a promotion on the basis of the result of performance evaluation.

4. This process is also effective in determining the effectiveness of the training programs conducted by the organization for the employees. It can show managers how much an employee has improved after the training. This will give actionable insights to the managers on how to improve the programs.

5. It creates a competitive environment amongst the employees in a good way. Employees try to improve their performance and get better scores than their colleagues.

6. Managers use this as a platform to get first-hand feedback from employees to talk about their grievances and how to handle them.

7. Keeping year on year record of appraisals gives managers a very good idea what is the pattern of the growth rate of employees and which ones have a declining rate and what actions need to be taken to improve it.

Disadvantages of performance appraisal

1. If the attributes being used in this method are not correctly defined the data collected won't be useful.

2. Sometimes biases can be an issue in this system.

3. Some objective factors can be vague and difficult to pin down. There are no known scientific methods to measure that.

4. Managers sometimes are not qualified enough to assess the abilities of the employees, thus be detrimental to the

growth of an employee.

essentials of effective performance appraisal System

1. Mutual Trust: The existence of an atmosphere of confidence and trust so that both supervisor and employee may discuss matters frankly and offer suggestions which may be beneficial for the organisation and for an improvement of the employee. An atmosphere of mutual trust and confidence should be created in the organisation before introducing the appraisal system.

2. Clear Objectives: The objectives and uses of performance appraisal should be made clear and specific. The objectives should be relevant, timely and open.

3. Standardisation: Well-defined performance factors and criteria should be developed. These factors as well as appraisal form, procedures and techniques should be standardised. It will help to ensure uniformity and comparison of ratings.

4. Training : Evaluators should be given training in philosophy and techniques of appraisal. They should be provided with knowledge and skills in documenting appraisals, conducting post appraisal interviews, rating errors, etc.

5. Job Relatedness: The evaluators should focus attention on job-related behaviour and performance of employees. The results of performance rather than personality traits should be given due weight.

6. Strength and Weaknesses: The raters should be required to justify their ratings. The supervisor should try to analyse the strength and weaknesses of an employee and advise him on correcting die weakness.

7. Individual Differences: While designing the appraisal system, individual differences in organisations should be recognised. Organisations differ in terms of size, nature, needs and environment. Therefore, the appraisal system should be tailor-made for the particular organisation.

8. Feedback and Participation : Arrangements should be made to communicate the ratings to both the employees and the raters. The employees should actively participate in managing performance and in the ongoing process of evaluation. The superior should play the role of coach and counseller.

9. Post Appraisal Interview: A post-appraisal interview should be arranged so that employees may be supplied with feedback and the organisation may know the difficulties under which employees work, so that their training needs may be discovered.

10. Review and Appeal : A mechanism for review of ratings should be provided. Which particular technique is to be adopted for appraisal should be governed by such factors as the size, financial resources, philosophy'and objectives of an organisation.

various components of performance appraisal in HRM

Defined Goals and Objectives

An effective Employee Performance Appraisal system must have clearly defined goals in place to achieve task or objectives (OKRs). The goals need to be specific, clearly defined, measured and rated by points. This can be achieved through various input parameters formulated by the supervisors or managers, enabling the employees to improve in their job performance and to achieve their defined goals thereby contributing to the overall growth of the organization.

Managers and employees are always in sync when goals are defined clearly.

Ideal performance management system should also consider the complexity of goal or task performed by the employee.

Continuous Feedback

Measured and accurate feedback and reviews are important aspects of a good employee appraisal process. Employees love to have feedback not only from their immediate managers on the task assigned but also for their teamwork contributions, accomplishing multiple tasks/ projects handled by different departments. This would give a complete picture of employee contribution, so a 360-degree feedback would be the solution. Every employee should get accurate performance feedback about every aspect of task and work contribution from their supervisors, teammates, subordinates etc

Configurations Flexibility

Companies that strive and thrive for competitiveness and innovation, place appraisal system as an integral and continuous process in order to have productive employees.

Every organization has own rating scales or own appraisal methods to appraise or rate their own employees. So, employee performance management solution should provide configuration which would allow organizations to configure different KRA depending on job description.

Performance management application should also allow to imports tasks from JIRA, CRM etc.

Self Evaluation

Real-time Employee assessment should be in place right from goal or task creation to completion, self-assessment of a task, immediate supervisor and manager assessment, cumulative tasks rating, point in time rating. Employees who disagree with a rating should be given an opportunity to challenge the rating and get an explanation, if required, of how the rating was derived which might be questionable to him.

Having self evaluation as part of employee appraisal review and evaluation process enables employees to measure and gauge their individual performance of their tasks or goals accomplished, rendering significant achievements they get during any period of time, making them more accountable for their assigned tasks or goals.

This self appraisal should be the part of the overall performance evaluation that provides metrics to improve their job performance.

Compensation and Rewards

Every employee deserves the best compensation, rewards and recognition for their achievements. The compensation and rewards are substantiated with incentives, bonus, variable pay and an increase in salary, rewards for key accomplishments and other monetary benefits. Some of these are guaranteed ones and some are not which should be clearly communicated to all the employees by their top-level authorities. Including employee engagement process with rewards increase motivation and productivity.

People Analytics

Data driven insights related to employees can help HR department or Human resource manager to take proactive decisions.

Analytics helps Human resource department in figuring out how good or bad is the relationship between manager or employee.

Performance and Analytics driven reports also help in reducing attrition rate.

Performance improvement plan

Performance appraisal software should also include Performance improvement plan (PIP) for low performing employees.

PIP give low performers opportunity to improve for given time period.

Overall Assessment

Employee Performance management application should contain setting of tasks/goals self evaluation, immediate supervisor or manager feedback, performance rating and progress on the goals, constructive feedback, people analytics, compensation management and reward and recognition.

Also, effective performance management solutions should be easily to configure and deploy.

CHAPTER TWENTY-ONE

Employee Compensation/ remuneration

Compensation management, also known as wage and salary administration, remuneration management, or reward management, is concerned with designing and implementing a total compensation package.

Compensation is the **human resource management** function that deals with every reward individuals receive in exchange for performing an organizational task.

The consideration for which labor is exchanged is called compensation.

Compensation is what employees receive in exchange for their work. It is a particular kind of price, that is, the price of labor. Like any other price, remuneration is set at the point where the demand curve for labor crosses the supply curve of labor.

Employee Compensation/ remuneration

Everything you need to know about the employee compensation. Compensation or Remuneration is a systematic approach to provide monetary value to employees in exchange for work performed by them is called as compensation or remuneration.

Compensation may achieve several purposes assisting in recruitment, job performance and job satisfaction.

Compensation or Remuneration is a systematic approach to provide monetary value to employees in exchange for work performed by them is called as compensation or remuneration. Compensation may achieve several purposes assisting in recruitment, job performance and job satisfaction.

In the case of Human Resource Management, compensation is referred to as money and other benefits that are received by an employee for providing services to his employer.

Money and benefits received may be in different forms — based compensation in money or monetary form and various benefits, these may be associated with employee's service to the employer like provident fund, gratuity and insurance scheme and any other payment which the employee receives or benefits he enjoys in lieu of such payment.

R. Wayne Mondy defines compensation as, "Compensation is the total of all rewards provided to employees in return for their services. The overall purposes of granting compensation are to attract, retain and motivate employees."

Gary Dessler opines, "Compensation means all forms of pay or rewards going to employees and arising from their employment."

Employee Compensation – 10 Main Objectives

1. To attract well-qualified and competent personnel.

2. To motivate them for higher levels of performance by making arrangement of incentive payments.

3. To retain the present workforce by keeping their pay levels at the competitive levels.

4. To raise the morale of workforce.

5. To establish internal as well as external equity. Internal equity refers to payment of similar wages for similar work. External equity means payment of similar wages to similar jobs in comparable firms.

6. To maintain the labour and administrative costs in line with the ability of the organization to pay.

7. To comply with wage legislation.

8. To project a good image of company.

9. To satisfy employees and to reduce the incidents of grievances, absenteeism and quitting.

10. To reward the desired behaviour such as good performance, loyalty, dedication, etc.

Components of employee compensation

Salary and wages

In a compensation package, these typically make up the single largest component. This comes as no surprise since they are what potential and current employees use as a common point of comparison. The person's experience and skills should determine the salary, with subsequent increases in the future depending on the employee's value, performance level and contribution to the company.

Bonuses

Employee bonuses are one common way employers provide performance incentives and are usually paid out annually, often at the end of the year, in a single lump sum. A formal way of doing this is through profit-sharing plans. However, these are often tied to the company's success versus for rewarding and compensating employees for their individual performances and meeting goals.

Federal/state pay requirements

State and federal laws are in place for protecting employees from bad employment practices that could negatively affect the employee's paycheck. There are minimum standards set via federal labor laws that employers are required to follow; state laws expand this protection in some cases. Employers are required by many states to pay the state minimum wage, which when compared to the federal wage, is a little more per hour.

The Fair Labor Standards Act (FLSA) requires employers to pay overtime (one-and-one-half times the hourly rate) to certain employees. Overtime is often due to employees who work over 40 hours in a week since it is measured not by the day, but rather by the week.

Providing a competitive package

Many employers offer a competitive package of employee benefits to attract and retain employees. Along with a competitive wage or salary, additional benefits are usually provided. Smaller companies might offer fewer components in the package; however, the majority of larger corporations, as well as most all public sector government employers, offer a competitive and extensive employee benefits package.

Long-term incentives

Part of a competitive package could include stock grants or stock options to serve as a long-term incentive.

Health insurance

Health insurance is fairly standard with medium to large-size companies and some small businesses. Health insurance offers great value to the employees and saves them money since it is employer-sponsored. This provides employees with peace of mind since they know they have coverage; even with existing health issues.

Life and/or disability insurance

This type of insurance will usually cost the employee less if purchased through the employer and is an option.

Retirement plan

A common practice for employers is to offer a 401(k) plan since it is less expensive than regular pension plans and fairly easy to administer. Employees have more control over how much they contribute and invest, which is why they like these plans. Many employers match the amount invested or at least contribute in some way. Smaller companies often try to have a plan in place for their employees but might not contribute any money to them.

Time off

Time off includes vacations, holidays, personal days, bereavement and sick days. For employers who are unable to offer competitive wages and salaries, they usually seal the deal by offering more time off. Some employers might not make any distinction between vacation, personal or sick days which allows the employee to schedule time off when needed throughout the year at their discretion.

Miscellaneous compensation

This type of compensation can include things like employee assistance programs that may offer anything from legal assistance to psychological counseling or company cars to company discounts. Some companies are becoming more creative with adding extra perks, such as weekly visits from a masseuse or an onsite barista.

Overall though, a competitive salary, 401(k) and health insurance remain the most common offerings that enable companies to attract and keep high caliber employees who contribute to their success.

Factors Influencing Employee Remuneration

A number of factors influence the remuneration payable to employees. They can be categorized into (i) external and (ii) internal factors.

External Factors

Factors external to an organization are labour market, cost of living, labour unions, government legislations, the society, and the economy.

Labour Market

Demand for and supply of labour influence wage and salary fixation. A low wage may be fixed when the supply of labour exceeds the demand for it. A higher wage will have to be paid when the demand exceeds supply, as in the case of skilled labour. A paradoxical situation is prevailing in our country-excessive unemployment is being juxtaposed with shortage of labour.

While unskilled labour is available in plenty, there is a shortage of technicians, computer specialists and professional managers. High remuneration to skilled labour is necessary to attract and retain it. But exploitation of unskilled labour, like, for instance, paying niggardly wages because it is available in plenty, is unjustifiable. The Minimum Wages Act, 1948, is precisely meant to prevent this kind of exploitation.

Going rate of pay is another labour-related factor influencing employee remuneration. Going rates are those that are paid by different units of an industry in a locality and by comparable units of the same industry located elsewhere. This is the only way of fixing salary and wage in the initial stages of plant operations. Subsequently, a comparison of going rates would be highly useful in resolving wage-related disputes.

Productivity of labour also influences wage fixation. Productivity can arise due to increase effort of the worker, or as a result of the factors beyond the control of the worker such as improved technology, sophisticated machines and equipment, better management, and the like. Greater effort of the worker is rewarded through piece-rate or other forms of incentive payments. This form of productivity, due to individual effort, cannot form a criterion of general wage payments.

Productivity arising from advanced technology and more-efficient methods of production will influence wage fixation. While productivity can be measured in terms of any one of the several factors such as capital equipment, materials, fuel and labour, what matters most is labour productivity. It is the relationship between the input of labour measured in man-hours and the output of the entire economy, or of a particular industry or plant measured in terms of money or in physical terms. It may be stated that productivity has only subordinate role in wage fixation. It can, at best, help determine fair wages.

Productivity linked wages may help utilize human resources better. This is particularly relevant to our country where productivity is low.

However, the argument that productivity would increase if it is linked to remuneration is hardly acceptable to labour and labour organizations.

Cost of Living

Next in importance to labour market is the cost of living.This criterion matters during periods of rising prices, and is forgotten when prices are stable or falling. The justification for cost of living as a criterion for wage fixation is that the real wages of workers should not be allowed to be whittled down by price increases. A rise in the cost of living is sought to be compensated by payment of dearness allowance, basic pay to remain undisturbed. Many companies include an escalatory clause in their wage agreements in terms of which dearness allowance increases or decreases depending upon the movement of consumer price index (CPI).

Labour Unions

The presence or absence of labour organizations often determine the quantum of wages paid to employees. Employers in non-unionized factories enjoy the freedom to fix wages and salaries as they please. Because of large-scale unemployment, these employers hire workers at little or even less than legal minimum wages.

An individual non-unionized company may be willing to pay more to its employees if only to discourage them from forming one, but will buckle under the combined pressure from the other non-unionized organizations. The employees of strongly unionized companies too, have no freedom in wage and, salary fixation. They are forced to yield to the pressure of labour representatives in determining and revising pay scales.

Labour Laws

We have a plethora of labour laws at the central as well as at the state levels. Some of the central laws which have a bearing on employee remuneration are the Payment of Wages Act, 1936; the Minimum Wages Act, 1948; the Payment of Bonus Act, 1965; Equal Remuneration Act, 1976; and the Payment of Gratuity Act, 1972. The Payment of Wages Act was passed to regulate payment of wages to certain classes of persons employed in the industry.

It also seeks to protect workers against irregularities in payment of wages and unauthorized deductions by the employers. In addition, the Act ensures payment of wages in a particular form and at regular intervals. The Minimum Wages Act enables the central and the state governments to fix minimum rates of wages payable to employees in sweated industries. The Payment of Bonus Act provides for payment of a specified rate of bonus to employees in certain establishments.

The Gratuity Act provides for payment of gratuity to employees after they attain superannuation. The Equal Remuneration Act provides for payment of equal remuneration to men and women workers for same or similar work. The Act stipulated stringent punishments for contravention of its provisions.

In addition to legal enactments, there are wage boards, tribunals and fair wages committees which aim at providing a decent standard of living to workers. In fact, ours is the only democratic country in the world which has attempted wage regulation on so large a scale through state-sponsored agencies.

Society

Remuneration paid to employees is reflected in the prices fixed by an organization for its goods and services. For this reason, the consuming public is interested in remuneration decisions.

The Supreme Court, from its very inception, has had to adjudicate industrial disputes-particularly disputes relating to wages and allied problems of financial concern to the worker- an ethical and social outlook liberally interpreting the spirit of the Constitution.

Though the financial position of the employer and the state of the national economy have their say in the matter of wage fixation.

The Economy

The last external factor that has its impact on wage and salary fixation is the state of the economy. While it is possible for some organizations to thrive in a recession, there is no question that the economy affects remuneration decisions. For example, a depressed economy will probably increase the labour supply. This, in turn, should serve to lower the going wage rate.

In most cases, the cost of living will rise in an expanding economy. Since the cost of living is commonly used as a pay standard, the economy's health exerts a major impact upon pay decisions. Labour unions, the government, and the society are all less likely to press for pay increases in a depressed economy.

Internal Factors

Among the internal factors which have an impact on pay structure are the company's strategy, job evaluation, <u>performance appraisal</u>, and the worker himself or herself.

Business Strategy

The overall strategy which a company pursues should determine the remuneration to its employees. Where the strategy of the enterprise is to achieve rapid growth, remuneration should be higher than what competitors pay. Where the strategy is to maintain and protect current earnings, because of the declining fortunes of the company, remuneration level needs to be average or even below average.

Job Evaluation and Performance Appraisal

Job evaluation helps establish satisfactory wage differentials among jobs. Performance appraisal helps award pay increases to employees who show improved performance.

The Employee

Several employee-related factors interact to determine his or her remuneration. These include performance, seniority, experience, potential, and even sheer luck.

Performance is always rewarded with a pay increase. Rewarding performance motivates the employee to do better. Management prefer performance to effect pay increases but unions view seniority as the most objective criterion for pay increases. Experience makes an employee gain valuable insights and should therefore be rewarded. Potential is useless if it is never realized. Yet, organizations do pay some individuals based on their potential. Young managers are paid more because of their potential to perform even if they are short of experience. Some people have luck to be at the right place at the right time.

challenges of remuneration

Managing compensation is one of the most difficult aspects of being an HR professional, irrespective of the size of the company. Compensation professionals in the HR department face issues in determining the right pay and relevant perks that recognize and reward employees for the contributions they make to the company.

The operations and processing can take a huge chunk of your time. It is more pronounced in companies with a workforce that spans across different geographies. In smaller companies, the challenges are of a different kind; most small businesses are limited by budget and so the extent to which these companies can go to attract new talent in a competitive landscape while being fiscally responsible to themselves is small.

Let's take a look at the most common challenges when it comes to compensation management and how you can overcome them.

External competition

We live in an incredibly competitive world where businesses are willing to pay top dollar to get the cream of the crop talent. In order to attract and retain talent, your company must establish a compensation package that's on par with other companies in the same industry and location.

There are several market surveys to gauge the right pay for different roles. If you're constrained by budget, you can innovate by offering attractive vacation time offs, child care facilities, and other benefits that don't cause a dent on your budget.

Executive compensation

The many nuances of compensation management come into play when deciding the salaries of senior executives. This is particularly important for public companies that need to reveal the salaries of their top 5 employees which might not go well with shareholders and the general public. Even if that's not the case, the pay packages need to strike a balance between attracting good talent while being acceptable.

Internal equity

Take a pay review and we're sure you'll be surprised by the results. Even though the government and businesses strive to achieve pay equity, the wage gap persists. In fact, the World Economic Forum estimates that it will take at least 202 years to close the wage gap.

You should continuously assess your pay gap efforts and create awareness in the senior management to fix this issue. Managing gender wage gaps is something that's so close to our hearts so much so that we wrote a whole blog about it. You'll find it here.

Gaps in employee expectations

There's always a conflicting disparity between what the employee expects to be paid and what the organization wants to pay. And, the HR is stuck in between. Also, employees usually don't take into account the entirety of their compensation package. They only consider the net pay.

You can bridge this gap by providing total compensation statements to clearly communicate the value of their compensation in its entirety.

Lack of digitization

Managing compensation and communicating the outcomes is a very effort-driven task. When not done digitally, it can take up to several months from design to implementation and finally to communication and requires a lot of data crunching/ formulas/ sheets on Excel. Obviously, it's not the best use of your time nor skills.

Spreadsheets and legacy software force you to focus on administrative details, most of which can be automated by using online compensation management software like Compport. It can simplify your processes, save your time and resources, and enable you to design smarter, engaging compensation plans for your workforce. According to real-life examples with different Compport clients, it has been proven that Compport can bring in 95 percent more efficiency.

Closing thoughts

Your compensation strategy should be connected to business goals and financial data so you can get a complete picture of its effectiveness. When wrongly handled, it can cause a rift between employees and management. Though these challenges may seem daunting, proper planning and diligent efforts can help you overcome them. The right tools will help you move beyond manual work and transactions and focus on what's important–motivating your employees and building a great culture.

incentive

An incentive provides additional compensation for those employees who perform well. It attempts to tie additional compensation as directly as possible to employee productivity.

Further incentives are monetary benefits paid to workmen in recognition of their outstanding performance. They are defined as "variable reward granted according to variations in the achievement of specific results".

Incentive systems should be tied as much as possible to performance. If an incentive is actually to spur increased performance and effort, employees must see a direct relationship between their efforts and then- rewards.

Incentives can be short-term and/or long-term, which can be tied up with the performance of an individual employee or a group/unit's productivity.

Performance through incentives may be defined as cost saving, quantity produced, standards met or quality improved, revenue generated, return on investment or increased profit.

Meaning

The main purpose of incentive is to tie employees' rewards closely to their achievements. This tie is done by providing more compensation for better performance.

Individual will generally strive for additional rewards by higher production and their performance depends upon higher efforts. Some people may prefer some extra time off rather than more money.

An incentive provides additional compensation for those employees who perform well. It attempts to tie additional compensation as directly as possible to employee productivity.

Further incentives are monetary benefits paid to workmen in recognition of their outstanding performance. They are defined as "variable reward granted according to variations in the achievement of specific results".

The international labour office refers to incentives as payment by results. But it is appropriate to call them Incentive systems of payment'. 'Emphasizing the motivation i.e., the imparting of incentives to workers for higher production and productivity'.

Incentives – Importance

For all businesses, no matter the industry, maintaining morale is very important in order to ensure your staff are driven to work hard for your company. Businesses are beginning to adopt incentive schemes in order to help with the success of their business. So, why is offering incentives so important?

1. **Increases productivity**

Everyone knows that productivity is essential to ensuring your company's success. Productivity drives business, so what drives your employees? Incentives are a great way to ensure that your employees stay motivated to do their job to the best of their ability. By offering something they can achieve if they hit a certain target or achieve something, they have something to work towards.

2. Decreased Employee Turnover

Giving incentives to your employees not only motivates them to do their work, but it can also motivate them to stay longer at the business. Having these perks might be the reason they choose to stay at your company, instead of looking elsewhere.

3. Happy Employees

Not only are incentives great for your company they are also great for your employee's happiness and wellbeing. Allowing them to blow off steam or win prizes is a great way to ensure they are happy working for the company.

4. Help attract new talent

According to Glassdoor, incentives do attract talent, with 57% of candidates reporting it as one of their top considerations before accepting a job. To attract top candidates, you need to stand out from the competition and offering unique incentive schemes could do just that. It could be the reason a candidate chooses your company over another one.

5. Team Culture

It has been found that productivity improves by 20-25% in organizations with connected employees. If you are offering incentive trips or things that multiple people will be able to win or attend, then it can help with team bonding and strengthen the relationships between your employees. IRIS FMP's Incentive programme incorporates peer-to-peer recommendations and managers nominations and is great for team spirit. Allowing colleagues to nominate one another for rewards is empowering, as it demonstrates that they value each other's opinion.

Among other incentive schemes, IRIS FMP offers the chance for all staff to go on an incentive trip every year. This year we sent 25 of our staff who exceeded their targets or excelled in their work last year to Long Beach, California for the American Payroll Association Congress. As well as everyone working very hard on our stand, a fantastic vacation was enjoyed by all with lots of fun and food! We are proud to give back to our employees that have worked so hard for us so that we can celebrate the success together.

The following are the salient features of incentives:

i. Incentives are based on standards fixed for job performance.

ii. They are to be linked to work performance.

iii. They should not vary from person to person and from time to time.

iv. They should motivate employees for better performance.

v. They should be measurable in monetary terms.

Characteristics of a Sound Incentive Plan:

Since the underlying objective of an incentive wage plan is to encourage workers to perform with zeal and earn good wages, a sound incentive wage plan would have the characteristics as under-

1) The incentive plan should be simple and easily understandable by the employee.

2) It should be acceptable to all the interested parties.

3) The reward under the plan should be adequate and immediately paid.

4) The norm or standard upon which the plan is to be based should be fixed after careful work measurement devices, such as time and motion studies, work sampling, standard data etc.

5) The plan should be fair and just both to the employer and employees.

6) It should not cost unwarranted burden on the employer nor should it deprive the worker of his due reward for an increase in output.

7) Guaranteed basic or time rate should be established by job evaluation. This will give the workers a feeling of security about their earnings.

8) There should be no unwarranted rate cutting, otherwise the plan would fail and create resentment among workers.

9) The incentive scheme should be definite and should not be changed frequently.

10) To avoid development of grievances among certain workers, the plan should be applicable to all jobs for which incentive plan can be profitably adopted.

Fringe Benefits

Fringe benefits are the additional benefits offered to an employee, above the stated salary for the performance of a specific service. Some fringe benefits such as social security and health insurance are required by law, while others are voluntarily provided by the employer.

Examples of optional fringe benefits include free breakfast and lunch, gym membership, employee stock options, transportation benefits, retirement planning services, childcare, education assistance, etc.

One of the advantages of fringe benefits is that they are tax-exempt for the employer, provided that the set conditions are met. On the contrary, the recipients of fringe benefits are required to include the fair value of the benefits in their annual taxable income.

Generally, fringe benefits are provided by the employer, even if the actual provider is a third party. This is because the employer is the party that pays for the benefit that is provided to the employee. Similarly, the employee is usually the recipient of the benefit, even if its use is extended to other family members.

How Fringe Benefits Work

The various fringe benefits that are provided to employees vary from one company to another, since the employer can choose the benefits that will be provided to employees during a certain period. Employees are given the chance to select the fringe benefits that they are interested in during recruitment.

Whether they are interested in a company car, taking an employer-paid gym membership or education financial assistance, the employee is at liberty to take the options that provide maximum comfort at their current position in the company. With retail employers, employees may also be provided with employee discounts, gifts, and no-additional-cost services.

Although the goal of providing fringe benefits to employees is to ensure their comfort at the workplace, it also helps the company stand out for potential employees. In highly competitive markets, employers may find it challenging to retain top employees on salary alone. Fringe benefits serve as additional compensation.

Providing unique fringe benefits to employees helps the company stand out from its competitors. It provides a greater opportunity to attract high value and talented employees from schools or from competing companies.

Types of Benefits

Fringe benefits can be categorized into two categories. Some benefits are required by law and others are provided at the employer's discretion.

1. Fringe benefits required by law

The mandatory fringe benefits are intended to provide employees with medical care, mitigate them from economic hardships in the event they lose employment, and provide them with retirement income to sustain them during retirement. The following are some of the mandatory fringe benefits that employers are required to provide:

Health insurance

This fringe benefit is contained in the Patient Protection and Affordable Care Act. It requires businesses that employ more than 50 people to provide healthcare plans, and employees are required to have health insurance coverage. The health care plans cover visits to primary care physicians, specialist doctors, and emergency care.

Unemployment insurance

The Federal Unemployment Tax Act (FUTA) requires employers to pay a federal and state unemployment tax to the Department of Labor, which provides wages, training, and career guidance to employees who become unemployed due to no fault of their own. Such benefits are meant to provide brief monetary assistance to unemployed citizens who meet the requirements of the act.

Medical leave

Businesses that employ over 50 employees are required by law to provide family and medical leave to an employee who has worked for over one year in the company. The medical leave is unpaid, protected, and can last up to 12 weeks.

Worker's compensation

The worker's compensation benefit is administered by the Department of Labor to federal workers who are injured at their workstation or acquire an occupational disease. Employees are provided with medical treatment, wage replacement benefits, rehabilitation, and other benefits. The compensation requirements vary by state, and injured employees should contact their state worker's compensation board.

2. *Fringe benefits not required by law*

The following benefits are provided at the employer's discretion. On the side of the employer, most of these benefits are taxable, but with certain exceptions. Examples of these fringe benefits include:

- <u>Stock options</u>
- Disability insurance
- Paid holidays
- Education reduction
- Retirement planning services
- Life insurance
- Paid time off
- Commuter benefits
- Achievement awards
- Fitness training
- Employee discounts
- Meal plans

Why Employers Offer Fringe Benefits

The following are some of the reasons why employers invest in fringe benefit programs:

Public perception

Companies that offer additional benefits above the salary often stand out from their competitors, and it makes the company attractive to different stakeholders. For example, customers are likely to buy from companies that are recognized in the public arena for treating their employees right and creating a safe place to work. The company will also attract talented workers who are looking to join organizations that value their employees.

Employee wellness

Companies lose money when employees are unable to work due to work-related illnesses and injuries. This is because the employees will spend time seeking treatment when they would have been offering their skills and experience to the company. Creating a safe working environment and providing fringe benefits such as gym membership, health insurance, and dental care coverage can improve their health and reduce sick leaves.

Employee engagement

Employees often work harder when they feel that the employer appreciates their contribution to the company. One way to increase employee satisfaction is by providing additional benefits like paid holidays, health care insurance, employer-provided car, stock options, etc. It will help reduce incidences of a disgruntled workforce and keep the employees engaged.

Additional Resources

CFI is the official provider of the global Financial Modeling & Valuation Analyst (FMVA)™ certification program, designed to help anyone become a world-class financial analyst. To keep advancing your career, the additional resources below will be useful:

- Commission
- Employee Morale
- Stock-based Compensation
- FMVA Compensation Guide

FMVA certification program

Advance your career in investment banking, private equity, FP&A, treasury, corporate development and other areas of corporate finance.

The fringe benefits offered by various organisation in India may be following types:

1. Hours of Work – As per Section 15 of the Factories Act, 1948, that no adult worker shall be allowed to work in a Factory for more than 48 hours in a week and more than 9 hours in a day.

2. Rest Period – Tea break or coffee break are allowed during the day to allow the worker to rest.

3. Holidays – As per the Factories Act, 1948, an adult worker shall have weekly paid holiday in general on Sunday or any other day in a week.

4. Shift Premium – Shift premium to the workers who are required to work during second and third shifts in a day.

5. Paid Vacation – Workers are eligible for paid vacation from 15 days to 30 days in a calendar year.

6. Holidays Pay – Independence Day, Republic Day, Gandhi Jayanti, Deepawali, Dusshera, Holi, Id and Christmas are gazetted paid holidays. Generally organizations after double the normal rate of the salary if the workers worked during these holidays.

7. Sick Leave – The employees are entitled to get full day when he is out of work due to sick for a 10 days in a calendar year.

8. Maternity Benefit – The Women are entitled to maternity leave for 12 weeks (six weeks before the delivery and six weeks after the delivery) in addition to cash benefit of 75 paise per day or twice of sickness benefit, whichever

is higher.

9. Disable Benefit – The employees are entitled to get the benefit under Workmen's Compensation Act 1923, if he is disabled temporarily or permanently (partial or total) during employment injury or occupational diseases.

10. Absence Leave – The pay is provided to an employee if he is absent from the work place due to the participating in training and development programmes.

11. Canteens – Fully or partially subsidized food and refreshments is provided to the employees during working hours.

12. Transport Facilities – Many organizations are providing conveyance facilities to employees from their residence to work place and back.

13. Housing Facilities – The big houses are providing company owners housing or subsidized housing facilities to their employees.

14. Purchasing Facilities – Many of the large organizations has set up the consumer stores in the employee's colonies and supply all essential goods and services at fair prices.

15. Educational Service – Educational services include tuition fees refunds, scholarships, setting up of schools and colleges, libraries and many more. These facilities not only provide to the employees of the organisation but also to their family members.

16. Medical Facilities – These include clinics, hospitals and counselling services. It reduces tiredness, absenteeism and employee turnover.

17. Financial and Legal Aid – Many organizations are provided loan funds, income-tax service, assistance in legal matters and group insurance plans to their employees.

18. Recreational Facilities – Organisations provide social clubs, arrange parties and picnics, reading rooms, libraries and entertainment programmes for their employees.

19. Travel Concessions – Many organizations are providing leave and travel concessions one time in a financial year to their employees.

20. Miscellaneous – Many organisations are providing other benefits to their employees such as Dipawali gifts, birthday gifts, pooja gifts and productivity or performance rewards, etc.

Importance for Employees:

The benefits are important to the employees for the following main reasons:

(i) They enhance the real earnings of the employees and enable them to save money, which they would, otherwise, have spent in the absence of these benefits.

(ii) Money value of these benefits has, for long, not been taxable under income tax law, thus enhancing employees' living standards. However, during more recent years, the value of these benefits is adjusted in the income tax payable by individual employees, but many of these still do not come into the ambit of income tax deductions.

(iii) Availability of the social security benefits in the event of such contingences as unemployment, sickness, disability, old age, maternity and so on mitigates the worries of the employees regarding apprehended insecurity.

(iv) Many benefits, particularly medical and refreshment facilities, are conducive to the protection of health of employees and enhancement of their efficiency.

(v) Housing accommodation with ancillary amenities and transport facilities result in saving of time and add to employees' convenience.

(vi) Many benefits are made available to the employees' family members, which promote congenial family life and strengthen employees' motivation.

(vii) Many companies make available to their employees plots for construction of houses or flats on lease basis, and also bear a part of the burden of interests on house loans. Thus, a major item of worry of the employees is mitigated.

(viii) Some companies advance loans to their employees on liberal terms for the purchase of vehicles and household appliances. This facility also raises the living standards of employees.

Importance for Employers:

Fringe/employee benefits are advantageous to the employers for the following main reasons:

(i) Employers have, for long, been enjoying substantial rebate on these benefits under income tax law. This advantage has, however, increasingly diminished during more recent years. Nonetheless, employers still receive rebates for expenditure on many of these benefits.

(ii) In establishments facing chronic problems of unstable workforce and absenteeism, long-term social security benefits such as life insurance cover, provident fund and pension and housing accommodation have proved effective in reducing their incidence.

(iii) These benefits generally tend to strengthen employees' motivation and efficiency resulting in higher production and reduction of labour cost.

(iv) Many companies have experienced establishment of sound employee and industrial relations as a result of provision of these benefits, especially when these benefits have emanated from agreement with the union.

(v) In some cases, the companies have been able to keep wage-rates at a low level on the ground of providing substantial benefits to their employees.

(vi) Provision of these benefits also enhances the prestige of the company in the community and enables competent workers to be attracted towards the company.

Fringe/employee benefits are also significant for the community and economy. It was during the Second World War period in the USA that the concept of "fringes" emerged in the context of compensation. The War Labour Board, which was entrusted with the responsibility of controlling wage increases, allowed fringe benefits holding that these would not stand in the way of measures intended to prevent inflation.

Even today, such a premise holds well in the situation of inflationary pressure under which "wages chasing prices and prices changing wages" is a usual phenomenon. Availability of fringe benefits diminishes pressures for wage increases which is helpful in fight against inflation.

Besides, many big companies have created infrastructure near workplaces in the form of housing colonies, roads, parks, lighting arrangements and community, educational and recreational centres. These benefit not only the residents of the locality, but also many others in the community. The facilities in the hospitals and dispensaries established and maintained by companies are generally made available to the public in the vicinity.

Marketing centres established by companies are similarly open to the public. Many other examples may be easily cited to show that the community derives advantages from the benefits intended to be provided for the employees.

https://annusehrawat8520.blogspot.com/

www.ingramcontent.com/pod-product-compliance
Lightning Source LLC
Chambersburg PA
CBHW020918160726
47993CB00005B/2025